MEZE

SNACKS, SMALL PLATES AND STREET FOOD
FROM THE MIDDLE EAST

SALLY BUTCHER

PAVILION

For Afi, for unlocking the doors of the Persian kitchen for me. And for Baba, for keeping our little Persian empire together. As in-laws go, they ain't bad.

contents

Introduction

Increasingly, formal dining is being nudged aside in favour of *meze*-style spreads: small plates or large platters of a wide range of (often simple) foods, shared in leisurely fashion.

At the same time, street food has come of age. In malls and farmers' markets across the land, food on the hoof has become a stylish and popular way to eat: sandwiches are getting a big makeover, pies are back in vogue, and even the Chinese takeaway is now as likely to have been cooked in front of you in a mobile wok as assembled secretly behind a door that always remains suspiciously closed.

It hardly needs pointing out that both *meze* and in all likelihood street food vending originated in the area conventionally known as the Middle East (and before you question my geography, I have deliberately wobbled over national borders, straying into neighbouring Greece, Sudan and South Asia). Street food is far from a recent innovation: in the Classical age, Greek and Roman writers alluded to open-air food vendors in the Mediterranean, and it is apparent that during times when not everyone had an oven or even a kitchen at home, there was a burgeoning market for such fare. These early takeaways were popular too with travellers, for whom they were often the only food option available.

But it is in medieval times that demand seems to have surged, and busy cities such as Cairo boasted an impressive array of specialised food vendors (collectively known as *tabbakhun*; it is fun to think that the little shop I run with my husband qualifies for the description as well, although I am not sure it will catch on) ranging from *halwaniyyun* (literally *halva* sellers) to *haraisiyyun*, who hawked *harisseh* (or *halim*: see p.66). In Turkey in the Middle Ages, takeaway kebabs were becoming popular, and Istanbul was already working towards its current position as one of the street-food capitals of the world. Pie stalls and dough-based treats evolved to sate the carb requirements of the poorer classes, many of whom, again, were without a bread oven at home.

Of course, it helps that most of the Middle East enjoys considerably warmer weather than northwestern Europe: this coaxes people out of doors and fosters street culture and politics, both of which need feeding. In fact, street food offers a fascinating snapshot of the social development of a nation. This is the case even in the diaspora: a survey of foreign takeaway restaurants and popular back home foods in London tells you much about the lands of origin therein. In Peckham alone, there are any number of street hawkers: our favourites are the quiet, anxious-looking man who wanders round with steaming boxes of spicy hot Afghan qorma in winter and the flamboyant West Indian drink vendor who appears on a bicycle in summer with a huge slab of ice and worryingly brightly coloured cordials.

Street food may have been the poor man's food of antiquity, but *meze* had altogether grander origins. The word *meze* (*mezze/mezedes*) is derived from *mazeh*, which is the Farsi word for 'taste', and the concept as a type of repast almost certainly evolved in the courts and eateries of Iran. The original idea was snippets or tasters of food to be eaten alongside and to mop up *arak*, wine or beer. It was clearly taken quite seriously, as Rumi refers to it repeatedly in his works, thus: '*Cook meze from tears on thy heart's fire; field and flower have been debauched by the clouds and the sun.*'

There is a rather wonderful but spurious tale that the whole 'taster' thing pertained to the custom among kings (who were undeniably more scandal-ridden and less secure than today's royalty) of having their food tasted lest it was poisoned. The sultans of the Ottoman Empire reputedly adopted the idea and the business of setting out a meal as a series of little platters took off from there. The conversion of much of the region to Islam did not put an end to the unhurried consumption of *meze* over a few drinks, but in the more devoutly Muslim (and thus non-drinking) nations it is now more often consumed as a selection of starters before a meal. Further west, however, in the Levant and Greece and Turkey, *meze* thrives as a major feature of the cuisine and a vast range of dishes have been created expressly with that style of eating in mind (many of them by the aforementioned Ottomans).

A celebration of comfort food

We may have become aware of the idea of comfort food only in the last couple of decades, but we have of course been cooking it for millennia: for the most part, it comprises the default dishes prepared by those who need a reminder of home, a culinary hug. The ritual act of preparing such familiar food is undoubtedly as soothing to the cook as it is to those who get to enjoy it. It is not about fast food, or fifteen-minute meals, or three-ingredient suppers, and in fact some of the dishes contained within these pages take quite a long time to prepare. My mother-in-law frequently spends a whole day preparing comfort food snacks for the week ahead. I am in a unique position to observe the phenomena, as my little emporium is located in a wonderfully cosmopolitan corner of London. The dishes my customers prepare are the stuff of childhood teatimes and family breakfasts, nutritious and usually cheap (a lot of it based on popular Ramadan recipes as there is no stronger focus on food than during the month of fasting).

Snacks, street fare and comfort food: this book is all about celebrating these less formal styles of eating.

Nuts and Nibbles

Torshi Shoor

MR SHOPKEEPER'S
PATENT PICKLED VEG

Useful Iranian pickle facts: *torshi* in Farsi just means 'sour pickle', but is often used as a generic term for pickles. *Shoor* specifically refers to ingredients preserved predominantly in brine, and *liteh* usually implies a type of finely minced, spicy *torshi*.

These chunky pickled veg make a great mini-*meze* dish, as they are effectively pickled crudités. Making anything that you sell in a shop on a regular basis demands a degree of consistency which Mrs Shopkeeper and her slapdash ways can rarely provide. Mr Shopkeeper, AKA Jamshid, AKA my Honey Bunny, is a much more organised sort of chap than I am. So when it comes to the business of following recipes and doing things in a uniform manner time and again, it is generally understood to be his department. Thus our house pickle, which is enormously popular, is made uniquely by him. This is his secret recipe. Shh – don't tell him I've shared it with you...

It makes enough for at least three jars: one for you, one for the neighbours, and one for the Autumn fair.

* Golpar seeds

That's Persian hogweed to you. It smells like old socks and has a pungent flavour, but works well in pickles. It is also ground and used as a spice in Iran, as it is a 'hot' food (Iranians believe that all foods have either 'hot' or 'cold' properties, and that if you eat too many of one or the other you will end up imbalanced). Golpar is sprinkled on lots of 'cold' vegetables, such as those served up as snacks in the Iranian bazaars, to reduce the, er, flatulence-inducing effects therein.

FILLS AROUND 3 x
800G/1LB 12OZ JARS
2 cauliflowers, separated into small florets
1kg/2lb 4oz carrots, chopped into
   1cm/½ in rounds
2 onions, roughly chopped
1 head of celery, cut into 2cm/¾ in lengths
3–4 hot green chillies, chopped
500g/1lb 2oz baby cucumbers, cut into
   1–2cm/½–¾ in rounds

6–8 garlic cloves, quartered lengthways
2 tsp whole golpar seeds*
2 tsp whole dill seeds (or use dill weed)
2 level tsp ground turmeric
2 litres/3½ pints/8 cups salted boiled water
500ml/18fl oz/generous 2 cups malt vinegar
1 bunch of fresh spring garlic
   (or 200g/7oz dried, soaked for 24 hours),
   optional

This couldn't be easier, just mix all the ingredients together and ladle into sterilised jars (see below) or a suitable (sterilised) plastic barrel and seal well. Store somewhere cool and dark: your pickle should be ready after about one month.

Sterilising a jar takes two seconds: just fill it with boiling water, sloosh it around and empty it, then leave it upside down somewhere to drain and dry. Sealing a jar is equally straightforward, but if said jar has a metal lid, a little clingfilm between the product and the lid should prevent an adverse reaction between the two.

Khiar Shoor

PICKLED CUCUMBERS

This is probably the most popular Iranian pickle. These posh, pert and piquant gherkins are nothing short of addictive. In Iran, they are a regular visitor to the dinner table, sliced into sandwiches, chopped into salads and enjoyed as an any-time snack. Please note they bear about as much resemblance to the fish and chip shop gherkin as Pennsylvania to Peckham. They are salty, often eye-wateringly spicy, crunchy and traditionally very small. In the summer, baby cucumbers can be found in Middle Eastern shops and many supermarkets, so get pickling...

FILLS AROUND 2 x
800G/1LB 12OZ JARS
1kg/2lb 4oz baby cucumbers (about
    3–6cm/1¼–2½ in in length)
3–4 sprigs of fresh tarragon

4–5 thin, hot chillies
4–5 garlic cloves
1 litre/1¾ pints/4 cups water with 4 tbsp salt
2 tbsp white vinegar

Wash and drain the cucumbers, tarragon and chillies, and peel the garlic cloves. Bring the water and salt to the boil, then take off the heat and add the vinegar.

Distribute the cucumbers, chillies, garlic and tarragon evenly between your sterilised jars (see p.10), cover with the cooled brine and seal. Store somewhere cool; this delicacy will be ready after a month, but reaches perfection after two.

Zeitoun

OLIVES, MARINATED FOUR WAYS

A bowl of olives is perhaps the simplest *meze* item of all. The strong flavours challenge the taste buds in a way that few other foods do, while for those of us who live in climes less warm, to bite into a flavoured olive is to sup of Flora and the country green: one is immediately, briefly, deliciously transported to, well, somewhere that isn't one's local high street or gastro-pub. Olives may be small and low on calories, but the sensual ritual of eating them can leave one feeling quite replete. There again, for the (guesstimated) 33 per cent of the population who actually loathe olives, they are of course the snack from Hades.

Most self-respecting delicatessen counters are heaving with ready-marinated olives, but it is so much more fun to create your own. Here are four slightly different ways to prepare them at home.

for Green Olives

Rinse and drain around 500g/1lb 2oz green olives in brine. Cut a small cross in the bottom of each (fiddly but worth it), then add one of the following marinades and leave overnight:

Mix around 2 tablespoons of extra-virgin olive oil with 1 teaspoon rosemary, 1 teaspoon dried savory (or thyme), 3 crushed juniper berries and a measure of raki (or ouzo, or pastis). Good with a glass of wine.

Toast (dry-fry) 1 teaspoon fenugreek seeds with 2 teaspoons mustard seeds until they pop. Crush the seeds in a pestle and mortar, then add ½ teaspoon asafoetida* (optional: or you can use ½ a grated onion and 1 minced garlic clove instead) and 2 tablespoons olive oil. Pairs well with *doogh* or *ayran* (AKA salted yogurt drink).

for Black Olives

Rinse and drain 500g/1lb 2oz Kalamata-style black olives in brine. Chop/mash 2 garlic cloves, around 6 anchovies, 6 sun-dried tomatoes and 1 tablespoon capers together, then add 1 tablespoon red wine vinegar and 1 tablespoon olive oil to the mix. Stir through the olives, chill and leave for a few hours. This is great on *meze* spreads, or in salads/on pizzas. Nice with a fancy aperitif.

Buy 500g/1lb 2oz salted Moroccan or Turkish-style olives (they're the oily, wrinkly ones). Crush 1 teaspoon rose petals together with 2 teaspoons harissa spice mix (p.21), then add 1 teaspoon chilli flakes and 1 tablespoon olive oil. Drizzle over the olives and mix well. Leave for a few hours before enjoying with a cold beer.

*A note on asafoetida

Ah. Asafoetida. Don't be put off by the smell. It is famously used in Indian cuisine as a substitute for garlic and onion, which certain castes are prohibited from eating. It is also used in the kitchens of Arabia, Afghanistan and Pakistan. It is collected as a resin, which can be ground into a powder or used whole (in which case it needs to be exposed to heat to do any good). Whatever you do with it, the most important thing to remember about it is that a little goes a long way.

It is perhaps most interesting when used as a remedy. Traveller Charles Doughty noted in his book *Travels in Arabia Deserta* that it is a 'drug which the Arabs have in sovereign estimation'. It has a slightly anaesthetising effect, and thus can be used for toothache and sore throats, but it is also (reputedly) good at treating flatulence, viral complaints, headaches, stress and menstrual pain. Boil a little resin (if possible) or a teaspoon of powder in a cupful of water and sip at it slowly, pinching your nose to escape the 'aroma'.

LEMON-ROASTED ALMONDS WITH SAFFRON

This is one of our most popular imported products in the shop: the salty citrusy flavour is impossible to resist. While you can always buy them from us, you can re-create the scrumdiddlyumptiousness of them in your own home.

MAKES A BOWLFUL
(WHETHER YOU SHARE
OR NOT IS UP TO YOU)
150ml/5fl oz/⅔ cup lemon juice (fresh
   is best, but you can cheat and use
   good bottled stuff)

½ tsp ground saffron steeped in
   150ml/5fl oz/⅔ cup boiling water
200g/7oz/1⅓ cups raw almonds
3 tbsp olive oil
1½ tsp sea salt
1 tsp citric acid (AKA lemon salt)

Mix the lemon juice and saffron water together. Spread the almonds out in a shallow dish, and trickle the juice-water over them, turning the nuts over in the liquid so that they are well coated. Leave them for around an hour, turning them occasionally.

After the time is up, drain the almonds and pat dry: unless you are at least a *rial* millionaire, I insist that you retain the saffron marinade in the name of thrift.*

Preheat the oven to 180°C/350°F/Gas mark 4.** Spread the almonds out on a small baking tray and bake them for around 10 minutes.

Next mix the oil and salts together in a bowl then tip in the hot almonds, stirring with a spoon to ensure that the nuts are all coated. Spread them back on to the baking tray and bake for a further 10–15 minutes, or until they are a rich golden brown.

Leave to cool a little before sampling: these dudes get really hot in the oven. I speak from burnt-tongue experience. They will keep for 2–3 days: after that, they start to go a little soft, so best just to eat them all up real quick.

*Tip
Keep it in a wee jar in the fridge. You can add it to fish, vegetables, salad dressings, roast chicken... Or just use it for more nuts.

**Note
As a serious food writer (ahem), I am undoubtedly meant to be writing about the proper way to do stuff, but look: between you and I, these work out just as well in the microwave. Instead of cooking them for 10 minutes followed by a further 10–15, just cook them for 3 minutes followed by another 5 minutes. Obviously all microwaves vary, so do check that they are 'roasted' to your satisfaction. They will seem soft at first, but crisp up as they cool.

ZA'ATAR-FRIED CHICKPEAS

The wise Mullah Nasruddin was living a frugal existence, subsisting mostly on chickpeas and bread. His neighbour, who was a vizier to the King no less, lived on fine repasts provided by the royal palace. Puzzled by Nasruddin's contentment, he told his neighbour one day, 'Nasruddin, if you too endeavoured to ingratiate yourself at court, then you would not have to live on such peasant fare.'

To which the Mullah replied, 'But, my dear neighbour, if you too learned to live on chickpeas and bread, then you would not have to spend your time bowing and scraping in such obsequious fashion.'

Chickpeas are really versatile: a great snack in their own right, they can also be used as croûtons in soup or salads, and they make for a pretty garnish for *houmous* (see p.106) and similar dips. They may seem humble fare, but they are full of tryptophan, which makes you happy: you should always listen to Nasruddin.

MAKES A BIG BOWLFUL

200g/7oz/generous 1 cup dried chickpeas, soaked for 6 hours or overnight

splodge of olive oil
1 tbsp sea salt
1 tbsp *za'atar**

Rinse and drain the chickpeas, then leave them until they are quite dry.

Heat a little oil in a frying pan and add the chickpeas, followed a minute or so later by the salt and spice. Cook, stirring constantly, for around 3 minutes before spooning out on to some kitchen paper to drain. Leave them to cool a little before tucking in. They will keep for a week or so in an airtight plastic tub – if you can leave them alone that long.

* A note on za'atar
This is the Arabic word for thyme, and is also a ubiquitous Arabic spice mix comprising ground thyme, sumac, salt and sesame. It is the latter that you need here.

Maghrebi Habas fritas
SPICED ROASTED BROAD BEANS

Anyone who has tarried a while in a Spanish tapas bar will be familiar with *habas fritas*: fried (or roasted) split broad beans. Totally addictive, but not very good for those with crowns or implants.

In this recipe we take your *habas fritas* and raise them against some very nice Moroccan spices to create the perfect nibble to have with a few drinks.

Drain and rinse the broad beans, then leave them to drain thoroughly.

Mix the olive oil with the spices and salt, then roll the hopefully-almost-dry beans in the oil, stirring well to ensure that they are all coated.

Preheat the oven to 170°C/340°F/Gas mark 3. Spread the broad beans out on an oven tray and bake them for around 30 minutes, or until they are crispy and golden brown. Leave to cool before sampling/sharing. These will keep a few days in an airtight container.

MAKES A BIG
BOWLFUL
200g/7oz/generous 1 cup dried,
    split broad (fava) beans,
    soaked for at least 6 hours
3 tbsp olive oil
1 tsp smoked paprika
½ tsp ground cumin
½ tsp ground ginger
½ tsp ground chilli
1 tbsp garlic salt

DRY-ROASTED GREEN PEAS WITH FENUGREEK

This is a very moreish and almost healthy way to enjoy a modicum of salt. You can use fresh or frozen peas for this.

Rinse the peas and leave to drain (or roll them on kitchen paper to dry). Mix the oil with the spices and salt in a bowl, then tip in the peas, stirring gently (so as not to mash it all up) to ensure that the peas are all coated.

Preheat the oven to 150°C/300°F/Gas mark 2. Spread the spiced peas out on a baking tray (one with edges) and pop them in the oven. After 15 minutes, turn the heat right down to 120°C/250°F/Gas mark ½, and allow your peas to cook for a further 45 minutes, turning them gently halfway through. Take the peas out of the oven and test one: it should be crunchy without breaking your teeth. These spicy peas will keep for a week in an airtight plastic tub.

MAKES A BOWLFUL
300g/10½ oz/scant 2⅔ cups
    common or garden peas
    (defrosted if necessary)
3 tbsp olive oil
1 level tbsp ground fenugreek
    seeds
1 tbsp cracked coriander seeds
1 tsp cayenne pepper
1 tsp paprika
1 tbsp celery salt (or sea salt)

SPICED VEGETABLE CRISPS

In an 'ideal' world peopled by shiny Suzy Homemakers, every house would have a little tub of these almost healthy root crisps ready for their hungry brood. This kind of snack exudes homeliness and wholesomeness. But don't let that put you off.

Vegetable crisps are dead easy to make and are useful in lunchboxes and on the *meze* table alike. The addition of some Middle Eastern-style spices just takes them to the next level. We might actually have to patent them...

In each case the quantities should give you enough for one big bowlful.

CARROTS WITH CARDAMOM AND CUMIN

Carrots, cumin and cardamom are a cosy threesome, oft found together on the pages of recipe books. It's a relationship that clearly works, so who am I to argue?

3 large carrots
1½ tsp ground cardamom
1 tsp ground cumin
½ tsp coarse ground black pepper
½ tsp ground sea salt
2 tbsp sunflower or rapeseed (canola) oil

Preheat the oven to 190°C/375°F/Gas mark 5.

Peel the carrots and slice them very thinly. A mandolin would be handy here, although I find them scary and dangerous. The dextrous among you may well be able to shave off decent slices with a vegetable peeler.

Mix the spices and seasoning together with the oil, then toss the carrots in the mixture, turning them over until they are all coated. Spread them out on a baking tray and bake for 6–7 minutes, or until they are starting to brown and curl at the edges.

Cool them on a wire rack – they will crisp up more as they cool. These are pretty addictive on their own, but also team well with *houmous* (see p.106). They keep for a few days in a plastic tub.

BEETROOT WITH GINGER AND GARAM MASALA

Beetroot and ginger go together like Aladdin and his lamp. They just do. The addition of garam masala into the equation gives these crisps an exotic extra something. Personally I eat these as fast as I can make them, but should you manage to retain some, they are perfect paired with tsatsiki. They also make a fancy accompaniment to fish or game dishes.

2 large beetroots	½ tsp salt
1 level tsp ground ginger	½ tsp ground black pepper
1 tsp garam masala	2 tbsp olive oil

Preheat the oven to 180°C/350°F/Gas mark 4.

Peel the beetroot and slice them as thinly as possible. Mix the spices and seasoning with the oil in a bowl, and add the beetroot, turning it until coated all over.

Spread the slices out on a baking tray (or two): it doesn't matter if they overlap a bit as they curl during the cooking process anyway. Cook for around 30 minutes, turning the tray around halfway through. Tip on to kitchen paper and leave to cool – they will crisp up once they are out of the oven. They should keep for a few days in an airtight container.

TURNIPS WITH DUKKAH

Turnips aren't widely seen in crisp form. This may be because they stay ever so slightly chewy, but to my mind this just makes them even more moreish.

3 medium turnips
1½ tbsp olive oil
1 good tbsp *dukkah**

* Dukkah: an Egyptian condiment
To make your own, lightly roast 1 tablespoon shelled hazelnuts (or almonds), 1 tablespoon sesame seeds, ½ tablespoon cumin seeds and ½ tablespoon coriander seeds, and then grind them together with some salt and pepper to taste. This will keep for 2–3 weeks in a sealed container.

Preheat the oven to 180°C/350°F/Gas mark 4.

Peel the turnips and slice them thinly with a mandolin or sharp knife. Drizzle over the oil and turn them over with your hands to make sure the slices are coated. Spread them out on a baking tray and bake for 15 minutes. At this stage, sprinkle them with the *dukkah* on both sides, then pop them back in the oven for a further 20 minutes, or until they are starting to turn a pleasant shade of golden brown.

Leave to cool on a wire rack. These are fine on their own, but also work well with dips or topped with smoked meat/cheeses. Eat within a day or so.

HARISSA POPCORN

An irresistible TV snack craftily designed to distract your mates/other half so you can grab the remote control...

MAKES A BIG BOWLFUL
100g/3½ oz unpopped popcorn
2 tbsp olive oil
2 tbsp Harissa Spice Mix (see below)

Pop the popping corn in a pan with a lid or in the microwave. Once it has stopped hissing and spitting, tip it into a bowl. Mix the olive oil with the spice mix and drizzle it over the popcorn, tossing it all together to ensure everything gets coated. Share around...

HARISSA SPICE MIX

This is a very secret recipe, so don't share it with anyone now, will you? You can actually buy similar products in shops now, but it is more satisfying to make your own. Once you have used this spice mix, it is quite hard to imagine cooking without it. I have not yet managed to incorporate it into salted caramel, but give me time...

FILLS A 300G/10½ OZ JAR
2 tbsp coriander seeds
2 tbsp green cumin seeds
1 tbsp caraway seeds

1 tbsp chilli (red pepper) flakes
1½ tsp garlic salt (garlic sea salt is better)
1 level tsp smoked paprika
1 tbsp dried mint

Toast (dry-fry) the coriander, cumin and caraway seeds in a frying pan, stirring constantly: they only need a couple of minutes. Set aside to cool a little.

After five minutes or so, toss the toasted spices with all the other ingredients, then whizz the mixture briefly in a coffee grinder in batches, or pound in a pestle and mortar. You don't want it to end up totally homogenised and powdered: some texture is desirable.

Store it in an airtight jar until you need it. Which I assure you will be quite often. Use on fish, chicken, salads, bread, pizzas, lamb, vegetables, popcorn...

Fishy Things

WARM BARBERRY AND POSH PRAWNS WITH LENTILS

MEZE DISH FOR 8
OR A STARTER FOR 4

250g/9oz/1¼ cups Puy lentils

100g/3½ oz barberries*

big knob of butter and dash of oil

around 16 really meaty king
    prawns (king shrimp),
    shelled and deveined

⅓ tsp ground saffron steeped
    in a splosh of boiling water

4 tbsp olive oil

1cm/½ in fresh ginger, minced

3 tbsp pomegranate molasses**

juice and grated zest of 1 lime

salt and coarsely ground
    black pepper

4 spring onions (scallions),
    chopped

½ bunch each of fresh mint
    and parsley, de-stalked
    and chopped

* Barberries

If you can't find barberries
(try your local Middle Eastern
store), then substitute with
cranberries in the winter, and
redcurrants in the summer.

** Pomegranate
molasses

There are now, amazingly,
quite a few varieties of pomegranate molasses from which
to choose, such is the trendiness
of this ingredient in the West.
In this context, an Arabic one
is a better bet: it is less dark and
gloopy and a little less sour.

This is one with real wow factor. Mind you, you show most people a plate of posh prawns and they get excited regardless of how you prepare them. I never cease to marvel at the popularity of all things shrimp-like.

There are quite a few traditional Middle Eastern prawn recipes, mostly from the area around the Gulf and the Mediterranean littoral. But some Muslims avoid them altogether owing to a continuing debate as to whether they are halal (some fish is, but each sect/mullah interprets the issue differently): many regard them as *makrouh*, which means they're frowned upon but not disallowed.

A more authentic *meze* dish might be simply prepared prawns cooked with butter, lemon and parsley – but this one will elicit far more oohs and aahs, and even the odd *mash'Allah* (a generic Arabic term of appreciation with religious overtones – literally: 'God has willed it').

Pick through the lentils (even big brands can still contain small stones) and place them in a pan of cold water. Bring to the boil and cook for around 30 minutes, or until they are just cooked. Drain and leave to cool.

Next check through the barberries, which can also contain half the countryside, and soak them in cold water for around 20 minutes. This will anable any residual sediment/ barbs to sink to the bottom of the bowl. After this time, carefully scoop the berries out of the water, squeezing the moisture out.

Melt the butter in a frying pan along with a splodge of oil (to stop the butter burning) and lower in the prawns. Sauté for around 3 minutes before adding the barberries (unless you are using pre-cooked prawns, in which case you can cook the berries and prawns at the same time), then cook for 2 minutes more, stirring constantly. Next, add the saffron water, mix well and take off the heat.

Whisk the 4 tablespoons oil, ginger, pomegranate, lime juice and zest, and seasoning together in a bowl.

Finally, mix it all together. Stir the prawns and barberries through the lentils, drizzle with the dressing, then finally stir in the onions and herbs. Serve while it is all still warm.

CANDLES INN TARAMOSALATA

**MAKES A BIG
BOWLFUL**
5–6 slices of stale white bread,
    crusts off
2 tbsp tarama paste (about
    80g/3oz), or 2 smoked roes
    (about 150g/5½ oz)
1 medium onion, cut into chunks
juice of 2 small lemons
200–280ml/7–9fl oz/
    ¾–1¼ cups corn oil
    (olive oil can be used but
    is really far too heavy for
    this dish)

Taramosalata: smoked fish roe dip, a lynchpin of Greek and Turkish menus in practically any taverna or *meyhane* anywhere in the world. And a strong contender for the title of the world's most fattening dish. Not that I want to put you off or anything. Trouble with taramosalata is that it is quite addictive: one of those foods that you just keep scoffing until you've had far too much.

I made so much of it during the years I spent working in Greek restaurants (including the Candles Inn of the title) that I used to dream in pink. Except of course real cod roe is not that brightly coloured and many chefs resort to colour to lend the dish its trademark 'chi-chi-ness'.

It is easy to make at home – if you have a blender (no worries if you don't – it will just take you longer). It is an emulsion, and so, like mayonnaise, relies on the gentle addition of oil to other ingredients.* The trickiest part of the whole operation is finding the smoked fish roe. In Greece carp or mullet roe is used, but the most common by far is cod. The good news is that all good fishmongers sell 'fresh smoked' cods' roe, and *tarama* paste (salted roe) is available in most Greek and Turkish shops. Note that the fresh roe does not have quite such a strong flavour as the paste and so you will need to use a little more.

Soak the bread in cold water for 10 minutes or so.

Put half of the *tarama* in a blender along with half of the onion and give it a quick whizz. Squeeze the water out of the bread and add half of it to the pink purée along with half of the lemon juice. Blend it for a good few minutes – you need the bread to be broken up and the paste to be distributed evenly.

Trickle the oil in very very slowly while the motor is running. Keep going until the mixture is thick, glossy and smooth and will absorb no more oil – the quantity of oil will vary slightly according to how big your lemons were and how much moisture was left in the bread, but it should be about 125ml/4fl oz/½ cup. Scoop the first batch out and repeat with the other half of the ingredients. If it curdles, don't despair: just empty the blender (retaining the contents), wash it and run it under cold water to cool it, then start a new batch using the curdled gunk in place of oil. It will be fine, promise.

Serve chilled: finely chopped dill or parsley and an olive are the traditional garnishes. Hot pitta bread is a requisite.

*

A note on
emulsifying
My father was a paint chemist, and I spent many a happy hour watching him mix paints in his workshop. Nothing proved more satisfying than watching stuff emulsify, and the same principle is true in the kitchen. I still do a little happy dance every time I manage to make a batch of mayonnaise without it curdling. Don't tell anyone, will you?

RENA SALAMAN'S PRAWN YIOUVETSI

Books about Greek food are myriad, but I only own one. (Actually, it's not even mine, but rather my mother's: I really should give it back to her one day, but I've had it for nearly 30 years so maybe she's forgotten, eh?)

When I worked in assorted Greek restaurants, Rena Salaman's *Greek Food* was my constant companion. Her anecdotal and highly informative style of writing truly transports the reader to the window of the *taverna* kitchen, and the recipes are as authentic as you will find anywhere.

The dish of *yiouvetsi* gets its name from the brown earthenware dish in which it is cooked: lamb and chicken *yiouvetsi* are also common. This is a lovely summery, light *meze* dish: very Mediterranean. Ms. Salaman writes of supping on *yarithes yiouvetsi* while overlooking 'sleepy interlocking emerald bays bordered by white luminous sandy beaches and dense pine trees reflected in the still waters'. Don't fret: I'm sure your dining room will be just as evocative. This is her recipe, with slightly increased quantities...

MEZE FOR 8
OR STARTER FOR 4
OR SUPPER FOR 2

500g/1lb 2oz shell-on raw king or tiger prawns (king or jumbo shrimp) – you can use cooked, shelled ones, if you are in a hurry
1 large onion, finely sliced
2 garlic cloves, minced (my addition)
120ml/4fl oz/½ cup olive oil
2 tsp dried oregano or thyme
1 glass white wine
500g/1lb 2oz fresh tomatoes, skinned and sliced (or use equivalent canned)
salt and freshly ground black pepper
big handful of chopped parsley
200g/7oz feta, thinly sliced

Preheat the oven to 180°C/350°F/Gas mark 4.

Blanch the prawns in just a little boiling water for around 3 minutes before draining them and reserving the cooking liquid. Set the prawns aside while you make the sauce.

Fry the onion and garlic in the olive oil, then add the herbs, wine, tomatoes and a few tablespoons of the prawn cooking stock. Season to taste and simmer gently for a couple of minutes.

When the prawns are just cool enough to handle, shell all but four of them. Next, devein them if needed: if they have a black streak down the back, just pull it away with a sharp knife (the black vein is their 'wastage system' and is best not eaten). The four reserved prawns should be shelled and deveined, but leave the heads and tails intact.

Arrange the prawns in one large or four small *yiouvetsi* (oven dishes), propping the ones with the heads still on against the side of the dish so it looks as if they are peeking over the edge (just for fun, like). Pour the sauce over the seafood, sprinkle it liberally with parsley and spread the feta over the top. Bake for around 20 minutes.

Enjoy with warm bread, and maybe dig out that old *bouzouki* CD you brought back from your holidays.

STREETWISE SARDINES

MEZE FOR 6

6 large fresh whole sardines,
scaled and gutted

olive oil

salt and freshly ground
black pepper

3 tbsp chermoula (optional:
see bonus recipe below)

6–12 vine leaves,
depending on size

lemon wedges

The sardine is perfectly designed for snacking. It's easy to pull apart, highly nutritious, and when it's cooked properly, so very tasty. Therein lies the rub: there are so many badly cooked sardines being dished up all over the world that it is quite off-putting. The chief problem is that they are usually over-cooked or cooked from frozen, which leads them to disintegrate rather swiftly. I have also been served sardines that are burnt on the outside and raw in the middle, and those that have been improperly cleaned and not exactly fresh. The trouble is that once you have eaten something that is perfectly prepared, it is hard to accept second best: anyone who has eaten smoky, freshly grilled, lemon-squeezed sardines with their fingers while strolling the chattering evening streets of anywhere warm-by-the-sea will understand what I mean.

The secret is to use very fresh fish. Frozen are just about acceptable if you defrost them properly. The other secret is to wrap them in vine leaves: this stops them from burning, helps the fish remain moist, and makes them easier to deal with should you wish to do that warm-by-the-sea thing and eat it with your fingers while walking round the garden.

They are lovely grilled without any extra flavouring, but I offer you the *chermoula* option for when you are cooking for pernickety 'oh it smells/tastes fishy' types.

Drizzle the sardines with olive oil inside and out, and gently rub in some salt and pepper. If using *chermoula*, fill the cavity with the rub and marinate at room temperature for around 30 minutes before cooking.

If you are using fresh vine leaves, blanch them for 2–3 minutes before using: if you are using preserved vine leaves, give them a quick rinse before use as they are very salty. Wrap each fish in one big or two small leaves (the head and tail do not need to be covered), and brush the outside of each leaf with a little olive oil.

Preheat your barbecue or grill (alternatively, you can bake these in an oven preheated to 200°C/400°F/Gas mark 6) and cook the fish for around 3 minutes on each side (or around 20 minutes in the oven). The traditional thing of a fish being cooked when its eyes whiten holds true with sardines.

Serve with chunky bread (best for fish – it acts as an emergency aid should someone splutter on a bone) and lemon wedges, together with any surplus *chermoula* sauce.

BONUS RECIPE: *CHERMOULA*

Chermoula is a classic Moroccan sauce, although confusingly it has appeared on the market recently as a dry spice mix. It goes with just about any savoury dish, especially fish, and is easy to whizz together. Just blend or pound together half a bunch of fresh corian-der, 1 tablespoon paprika, 1 teaspoon chilli flakes, 1½ teaspoons ground cumin, 3 garlic cloves, ¼ teaspoon ground saffron, grated zest and juice of ½ a lemon and 2½ tablespoons olive oil. Use as a marinade, rub or to drizzle on stuff. Will keep for a week in the fridge.

ANCHOVY LOLLIPOPS (*BANDERILLAS*)

Now I reckon snacks on cocktail sticks are due for a comeback. After all, Black Forest gateau, jumpsuits, lava lamps and cupcakes have all discovered renewed trendiness. Cheese and pineapple can't be far behind...

These little numbers are based on the Spanish *tapas* idea of *banderillas* (named after matadors' stabby things), but have an extra Middle Eastern twist. They are so simple I feel slightly embarrassed presenting this as a recipe: it is more a serving suggestion than anything else.

While I am sure you have better things to do with your day than scour hardware stores measuring their cocktail sticks, it is worth trying to source slightly longer ones for this recipe.

MAKES 12

12 quails' eggs

2 tsp *za'atar*

12 baby Turkish-style pickled chillies

14 nice pitted olives (garlic stuffed would be cool)

6 Iranian pickled cucumbers (you could use the ones you made on p.12), halved horizontally

12 plump anchovies (the ones in vinegar work best here as they are firmer)

handful of large coriander (cilantro), parsley, basil and mint leaves

Boil the quails' eggs for around 4 minutes before peeling and halving them. Once they are cool, rub the cut face of each half in a little *za'atar* and sandwich them back together.

Thread all the ingredients, interspersed with bits of herb, onto 12 cocktail sticks. The anchovy should be folded concertina-style. And that's it: a cracking little munch, offering soft, crispy, salt, sour, spicy, umami and plenty of colour.

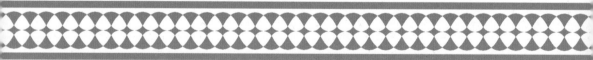

Psaria

GREEK-STYLE FRIED FISH WITH VINEGAR SAUCE

Seminal seafood meals are invariably rendered thus by the experience of sitting by the sea, watching the sun play on the water, maybe dangling a toe in the briny and patently not being at work. But the good news for those of us trying to recapture that whole thing at home is that the other secret of great seafood is that 'less is more'. The best fish I have ever eaten has been the most simply prepared: and nowhere do they understand this better than in Greece.

The most popular and common way to cook fish is to flour and then fry it. The beauty of the Greek and Cypriot approach is that it is not dependent on the type of fish: they will buy a bag of assorted fish and cook it all the same way. Chat to your fishmonger and ask which fish he recommends for frying: you want either small whole fish, or slightly larger ones, that have been filleted: baby mullet, sardines, herrings, mackerel and sprats are obvious choices.

The vinegar sauce is a traditional accompaniment and just adds a wee bit of tongue-tickling oomph.

CLASSIC MEZE FOR 4–6
800g/1lb 12oz cleaned, filleted (unless the fish are weeny) and scaled fish
salt
plain (all-purpose) flour (150g/5½ oz/ generous 1 cup should be enough)
1 tsp paprika
1 tsp ground turmeric

sunflower or rapeseed oil (corn oil is more authentic – but I find it a bit heavy)
3 garlic cloves
1 tsp fresh or dried rosemary
100ml/3½fl oz/scant ½ cup white wine vinegar
big handful of fresh parsley, chopped
freshly ground black pepper

Wash the fish and dry with kitchen paper before sprinkling it with salt. Mix 3 tablespoons of flour with some more salt, along with the paprika and turmeric. Coat each piece of fish with the flour mix and shake off any excess (sift and reserve any flour that is left over).

Next heat about 1.5cm/⅝in of oil in a frying pan and fry the fish for around 2 minutes on each side, or until they are golden brown; once they are cooked, transfer them to an ovenproof dish.

Strain around 3 tablespoons of the cooking oil into a saucepan and bring it back to sizzle point. Toss in the garlic and rosemary, then add around 1½ tablespoons of flour (using the flour you collected above), stirring well so it forms a roux. Add the vinegar slowly, plus a little water if it still looks very thick, then add the parsley and season to taste.

Finally, pour the sauce over the fish. You can serve the fish as it is, but more tradition-ally the dish is left to cool for an hour or so and served at room temperature or chilled: this enables the flavours to mingle and get to know each other.

Oolonganch Litsk
ARMENIAN STUFFED MUSSELS

Much of the Muslim world regards shellfish (and any seafood without scales) as *haram* or taboo. This means that the consumption of mussels is not that widespread, but in Armenia and Turkey they are really popular as street food and *meze* dishes.

I have to admit that I was a bit puzzled by the popularity and diversity of shellfish recipes in Armenia: it is, after all, landlocked and not particularly well stocked with freshwater species. But Armenia has shrunk over the millennia, and it previously boasted both a Caspian Sea littoral and easy access to the Black Sea and the Mediterranean. The Turks, of course, have a huge coastline and a long-standing love of seafood.

MEZE FOR 6

18–24 large fresh mussels, cleaned and debearded

salt

75g/2¾oz/scant ½ cup currants

1 large onion, chopped

knob of butter

75g/2¾oz/½ cup pine nuts

1 tsp ground allspice

1 tsp dried dill

salt and freshly ground black pepper

125g/4½ oz/½ cup pudding (or any short-grain) rice

big handful of fresh parsley, chopped

olive oil

juice of 1 lemon

Place the mussels in a bowl of lukewarm salted water and leave for 30 minutes, or so: this tricks them into opening, whereupon you can disarm their closure mechanism, thus making you feel like a piscatorial James Bond. You should also soak the currants.

Next, fry the onion in a blob of melted butter: once it becomes translucent, add the pine nuts, spice, dill and a little seasoning, followed by the rice. Take off the heat and stir the parsley through the mixture.

Now take each mussel in turn and, using a small knife, gently prize them open from the fat end towards the pointy bit: you are aiming to sever the ligament at the pointy end, but you want the shell halves to remain attached. Once done, wash the mussels again in cold water.

Spoon a little of the rice mixture (about a dessertspoonful) into each mussel, press the shell together and arrange them carefully in a saucepan. Place a plate on top of the shellfish, then add a good slosh of olive oil together with the lemon juice and enough water to cover the mussels. Bring the contents of the pan to the boil, then turn down the heat and simmer for around 45 minutes. Take off the heat and serve the mussels with extra lemon wedges. I like these hot, but they are traditionally served at room temperature and may also be enjoyed chilled.

TUNISIAN TUNA BRIK

Brik is derived from the Turkish word *boregi*, but basically we are talking pie here. Fish pie.

This book would not have been written had things turned out differently on a package holiday to Tunisia when I was 13. Any of you got a 13-year-old daughter? Sheesh, they can be obnoxious at times. Anyway, as an effort to persuade me to behave, my father totally convinced me that he had been offered six camels to leave me in the *souk*. It worked.

While our hotel food on that trip was memorable for all the wrong reasons, the street food of Sousse and Tunis was astonishingly good. These little fish pies stood out in my memory for flavour, plus they contain a delightful surprise.

They are traditionally made with a special thin, elastic pastry called *oarka*: this is hard to find in the West, but spring roll wrappers (or filo pastry at a pinch) make a great alternative.

MAKES 4

1 large onion, chopped
sunflower oil, for frying
1 small can (200g/7oz) tuna (sustainable,
    of course), drained
100g/3½ oz/½ cup pitted green olives,
    chopped
1 tbsp capers

2 tbsp chopped fresh parsley
1 tbsp chopped fresh mint
freshly ground black pepper
4 sheets *brik* pastry (*oarka*)
    or 4 spring roll wrappers (egg roll skins)
4 smallish eggs,
    plus 1 beaten egg if using *brik* pastry

Fry the onion in a dash of oil until it softens, then take off the heat and stir in the tuna, olives, capers, herbs and black pepper.

Stretch the pastry or spring roll wrappers out on a clean board. Put a quarter of the tuna mixture on one half of each sheet, making a well in the centre of the mix. Now crack an egg into each well before folding the other half of the pastry carefully over the tuna (to form a semi-circle or triangle, depending on the pastry you're using). Crimp the edges of the pastry with wet fingers to seal each 'parcel'. If you are using *brik* sheets, which are bigger than spring roll wrappers, fold the crimp again and brush the edges with beaten egg, as they are otherwise reluctant to stick.

Heat about 1cm/½in of oil in a frying pan (or use a deep-fat fryer) and once it is sizzling, lower in the *briks* very-everso-gently. Cook them for around 2 minutes before turning them over and frying the other side for a further minute.

Remove the pastries from the oil, drain on kitchen paper and allow to cool a little before serving with plenty of lemon wedges. And serviettes, because if you are lucky, the egg will still be runny. Oh, and perhaps a cup of nice mint tea.

Kebab-e-Mahi

CASPIAN FISH KEBABS

An observation. When you are trying to compel those whose regular diet rarely includes fish on a voluntary basis, sticking the stuff on sticks and making it look like chicken is a manoeuvre of great culinary cunning. And one to which I have stooped on several occasions.

Chunky sturgeon kebabs are a stalwart of restaurant menus all round the Caspian: the more northerly nations (Russia, Kazakhstan) prepare it with yogurt and pomegranate paste, whereas Iranians are more likely to marinate it in saffron, onion and lemon juice (like the *Jujeh Kebab* recipe on p.44). What I have done here is to take a northern dish and give it a southern twist: this fenugreek and tamarind marinade is typical of the hot cities and ports of the Persian Gulf. And don't panic: if your fishmonger is all out of sturgeon, this recipe will work with any firm fish, such as monkfish tail, tuna, swordfish, conger eel or halibut.

MEZE FOR 8
1 tsp fenugreek seeds, coarsely ground
sunflower oil, for frying
1 tbsp chopped fenugreek leaves
    (dried or fresh)
1 good tsp tamarind paste
4 garlic cloves, minced
2cm/¾ in piece fresh ginger, peeled
    and minced
½ tsp salt

½ tsp chilli (red pepper) flakes
400g/14oz fish, filleted, skinned and cut
    into 3cm/1¼ in cubes

TO SERVE:
juice of ½ lemon
iceberg lettuce leaves

Fry the fenugreek seeds in a little oil for a few minutes before adding the fenugreek leaves; cook for a minute or so more, stirring regularly, then take off the heat. When the mixture has cooled a little, blend it with the tamarind, garlic, ginger, salt and chilli, adding a little oil to make it workable, and rub the resulting paste all over the fish. Either pop the fish in a plastic bag and let it sit at room temperature for 30 minutes, or pop it in the fridge to marinate for 2 hours.

When you are ready to serve, thread the fish cubes on to either presoaked wooden skewers or oiled metal ones and grill over hot charcoal (or under a preheated hot grill) for around 6 minutes, turning once or twice (the fish, not you). It is quite fun to serve this with lemon-drizzled iceberg lettuce leaves: *meze* munchers can then use a leaf to scoop up and wrap the fish, obviating the need for separate lemon wedges, cutlery and finger bowls. If you want to make a meal of it, these kebabs can be served over rice along with the Kebab Salad Mix on p.55.

SQUIDDLY DIDDLY TWO WAYS

Squid, right – it's such a well-designed food. It's easy to clean, fun to cook and perfect for snacking. It readily absorbs/goes with almost any flavour you throw at it. And it is full of protein, trace minerals (including selenium) and vitamin B.

You can buy frozen, pre-cleaned squid tubes from most supermarkets now, but fresh squid does have the edge on flavour and tenderness. If you are reading this with a slimy fresh squid in front of you wondering what to do, well... firstly, cut off the tentacles just above the knobbly bit

between the eyes. Next, locate the weird 'plastic' backbone inside the tube of the squid: edge your forefinger around it and grasp it between your thumb and said digit, wrapping the other fingers around the rest of the innards. You should now be able to pull the spine and all of that gooey squiddy doo-da stuff out. Finally, run some cold water into the tube to clean it, then rinse off the tentacles, and presto. Now at this stage you could just coat it in seasoned flour and fry it. Or you could try something a little different...

SQUID COOKED IN FIZZY ORANGE TAMARIND BATTER

Batter is great when made with fizzy stuff: beer, *doogh* (yogurt drink), sparkling water or fizzy pop. The slight citrus flavour of the 'orange' in this batter contrasts well with the tamarind, and they combine to make the squid rather special, and funky. And we could all do with more funky squid in our lives.

MEZE FOR 8
500g/1lb 2oz clean squid
3½ tbsp plain (all-purpose) flour
(or you can use spelt)
1 level tsp salt
½ tsp ground white pepper

200ml/7fl oz/generous ¾ cup orange
Fanta (or other fizzy orange drink)
1 tbsp lemon juice
1 tsp tamarind paste
oil, for frying (soya bean oil is cheap and
nice with fish)

Cut the tube of the squid into rings and toss it in some flour along with the tentacles.

Sift the rest of the flour and seasoning into a bowl. Mix the fizzy pop, lemon juice and tamarind paste together before beating it slowly into the flour, whisking to achieve a smooth, batter-like paste.

Heat 5cm/2in of oil in a heavy-bottomed pan (or use a deep-fat fryer). Once the oil is sizzling hot, dip the floured squid into the batter, then lower each piece into the oil. Fry for around 3 minutes before removing with a slotted spoon and draining on kitchen paper. Warning: the batter will be a very dark brown owing to the tamarind – do not panic.

Serve with *Ajvar* (see p.108), or some nice aioli (see bonus recipe on the right). Cold beer is an optional extra.

SAFFRON AIOLI
Aioli is basically mayonnaise but without the mustard. Another 'but' is that it is made with olive oil instead of just vegetable oil. The Spaniards' secret ingredient for a really thick end product is... mashed potato. To make, steep ¼ teaspoon ground saffron in a tiny splash of boiling water. Add the juice of ½ lemon, then either use a whisk or your blender to mix in 1 egg yolk, 4 garlic cloves, and a pinch of black pepper. Slowly add around 100ml/3½fl oz/scant ½ cup each light extra-virgin olive oil with 100ml/3½fl oz/scant ½ cup rapeseed (canola) or sunflower oil: aiming for a glossy, thick emulsion. Stir in 2 cooked, mashed (cool) waxy potatoes, beating well, a handful of fresh chopped dill and coriander (cilantro), and salt.

NICKY'S SQUID STIFATHO:
SQUID COOKED IN INK

Nicky has an innate feel for food, especially Mediterranean stuff. This recipe evolved during her summers spent working in Greece and many years spent head cheffing in a Cypriot *taverna*. She gets very excited about food, so if you can imagine this recipe recounted with lots of hand gestures and great gusto...

MEZE FOR 6
a good glug of olive oil
1 bay leaf
about a dozen peppercorns
4 or 5 cloves
30g/1oz cinnamon sticks
2–3 garlic cloves, minced
500g/1lb 2oz squid cleaned, dried and cut
    up into similar-sized pieces, or if they
    are babies you can use them whole

50ml/1¾ fl oz/scant ¼ cup red wine
a slosh of red wine vinegar
1 sachet (around 4g/⅛ oz) squid or
    cuttlefish ink*
tomato paste, to taste
salt

Tip
I add the salt at the end because sometimes the fish, and the ink, can be quite salty already. The paste helps give a better colour (it can sometimes look a bit grey and unappetising), thickens it slightly, and sweetens it too.

*Squid ink
Oh yes, now about the ink. If you buy fresh whole squid and it's large, you may find ink sacs inside them worth collecting, but the best ink comes from cuttlefish. This can be bought in sachets from the fishmonger or you could just make the whole thing with cuttlefish and harvest your own.

Make your saucepan really hot (put it on and leave it while you get your spices and garlic ready) then add the olive oil, quickly followed by the bay leaf, spices and garlic. Let them fry for a few seconds, being careful because they will pop and spit, then add the squid (which, if you really did heat the pan well, might make quite a frightening noise). Stir briefly, then when all goes quiet, add the red wine, a big splash of vinegar and the ink. Cover, turn down the heat and simmer until no longer chewy but still with a bit of bite, anywhere from 20 minutes to 1½ hours depending on the beast in question.

When it's cooked, add salt and a touch of tomato paste to taste and cook for a further 4–5 minutes. Serve with warm bread.

Meat On Sticks

Kebab-e-Koobideh

FEEDS AROUND 6

2 medium onions, peeled

1 kg/2lb 4oz really good-quality minced lamb (shoulder would work best: the kebab needs some fat in it to make it cohere)

2 level tsp salt (Iranians would use a lot more)

1 tsp ground black pepper

⅔ tsp bicarbonate of soda (baking soda)

2 tsp ground cumin (optional)

6 tomatoes, halved

TO SERVE:

6 flatbreads (preferably *lavash*)

ground sumac

This is the most basic-and-yet-popular of the Iranian kebab family. *Koobideh* means minced, and this is indeed a fat skewer of juicy minced lamb. It is perhaps the favourite food of all time among Iranians. Jamshid (husband person) actually dreams about this dish. When he's not dreaming of me, natch.

The first night I ever spent in my in-laws' home, I was fascinated by the fact that most of their dinner was cooked over a wooden fire in the fireplace, pride of place in the proceedings being given to this *kebab-e-koobideh*. The old fireplace is now covered by a fancy suite, but still when the mood takes them they will invite all the family round, push the furniture back and host an indoor barbecue.

It is in principle simple, the flavour coming from the correct blend of meat and onion, perfect seasoning and the fact that it is (ideally) cooked over a real fire. The only complicated bit about making it is getting it to stick to the skewers. Iranians love trying to teach the uninitiated how to do it, as it is such a great source of mirth to them. *Koobideh* are traditionally cooked on broad, flat skewers 2–3cm/¾–1¼in in width: if you don't have any flat skewers (most Iranian shops do sell them), just use two parallel thin skewers… or you can just do the whole thing without the skewers.

Light the barbecue or preheat the grill or oven to 220°C/425°F/Gas mark 7. Put the bowl end of 2 teaspoons in your mouth so that they cross over, then grate the onions. This is as close to non-crying as you can hope to get in the weepy world of onions: really, it works.

Mix the onion into the lamb and add the seasoning, bicarbonate of soda and cumin, if using. Pound the mixture well with your hands: generally the less you play with food the better, but in this case the mixture benefits from the warmth of your hands, as this causes the fat to soften and the whole thing to come together.

Using wet hands, mould the meat on to your skewers (these kebabs are usually made to around 18cm/7in long), allowing the impression left by your fingers to show – the kebab should still display these wavy crenellations once it's cooked. Pop your skewers on to a hot barbecue, under a hot grill or into the oven on a baking tray. They will need about 5 minutes a side to cook (longer in the oven).

If you don't have any skewers, just form the meat into sausage shapes and use a spatula to lift them on to your grill.

Thread the tomato halves on to (any old) skewers and grill them alongside the meat.

Pop a sheet of folded *lavash* (or other bread) on to a plate. As each of the skewers of lamb is cooked, lift the folded over part of the bread over the skewer, pressing it down on top of the kebab. If you exert enough gentle pressure, you should now be able to withdraw the skewer, leaving the kebab nestled in the bread. Add a couple of tomato halves, sprinkle with sumac, then tuck the ends of the bread in to make the kebab more wieldy.

These kebabs are just as often enjoyed with buttered saffron rice, when they become known as *chelow kebab. Noshe jan!* (Which kind of means 'enjoy!' and '*bon appétit!*' and 'you're welcome!' all in one expression.)

Tip

The secret in eliciting the maximum meaty enjoyment out of this dish is to let the kebab 'rest' for around 5–6 minutes after cooking, so that at least some of the juices from the meat soak into the bread. Of course, if you leave it for too long, the thing will become far too soggy.

Jujeh Kebab

SPRING CHICKEN MARINATED
WITH LEMON AND SAFFRON

Jujeh kebab is on the menu of every Iranian restaurant and kebab joint across the globe: its flavour is simply stunning and it would be easy to assume there is some trick or secret ingredient involved. There is not. It is truly easy to make, and the learning thereof will greatly enhance your barbecue cred.

This is one's other half's recipe. He is apparently king of the grill. All men believe that they have inherited the barbecue gene: Iranian men reckon they invented it. For this reason, you should never leave them alone with a box of matches: their inner Zoroastrian will come to life. Father-in-law has been found lighting fires (for the most part fairly safely) in the most ill-advised of places. The upside of this national tendency, of course, is that if you are ever shipwrecked with an Iranian male, he will at least be able to light a fire.

SERVES 4

2 x poussins, boned, skinned and chopped into
    4cm/1½ in pieces
2 onions, grated or very finely chopped
½ tsp ground saffron

⅔ bottle Iranian lemon or lime juice (which is
    somehow extraordinarily strong), or the
    juice of around 6 fresh lemons or 10 limes
salt and freshly ground black pepper
a dash of olive oil

It's a doddle; all you do is….

Place the chicken in a sealable container and add all the other ingredients. The saffron should be sprinkled on to a saucer of boiling water and allowed to cool before it is mixed in. You only need to add as much lemon juice as it takes to cover the meat, but this probably will be most of the bottle. Mix the ingredients well, cover and marinate overnight in the fridge.

When you are ready to cook, thread the chicken on to skewers and cook over fire if possible; although you can cook it in the oven (200°C/400°F/Gas mark 6) on a baking tray for around 20 minutes, or you can grill it for around 15 minutes, turning it from time to time.

Serve wrapped in warm flatbread with a pile of fresh herbs to replicate that downtown Tehran experience. Alternatively, you could always make it dinner food by popping it on a bed of basmati rice and serving it alongside fresh herbs, pickles and raw onion.

Kebab-e-Chenjeh
SHISH KEBAB

The story of the origins of *shish kebab* are somewhat apocryphal: the idea of tired and hungry hunters/horsemen roasting chunks of meat on the end of their swords is so logical it must be true, right? *Shish* is actually the Turkish and Armenian word for skewer, although the term *shish kebab* is now widely understood to refer to the dish of cubes of meat (invariably lamb or beef) on a skewer. *Chenjeh* is the Persian term for a kebab of this nature.

You would think that this would be the easiest, shortest recipe in the chapter. Like, put meat on stick and cook it. And it really is that simple... until you start investigating the great salt debate. After a great deal of 'serious scientific research' (a euphemism for lots of eating and reading), I have summarised my conclusions about salt and meat below; it should however be remembered that there is no hard and fast rule, as cooking temperatures and cuts of meat vary considerably.

1. Lamb is a fatty meat that benefits from a long and well-seasoned marinating period. A moderate amount of salt added to the mix will aid the breaking down of the fat in the meat and considerably improve the flavour. Seasoning immediately prior to cooking dries and toughens the meat. 2. Beef is less prone to desiccation and can be seasoned in advance or immediately prior to cooking; the latter seems best to enhance the meaty flavour. 3. Salt and souring agents, such as vinegar and lemon juice, do not work well when used together in a marinade.

So with all of this in mind, I offer you my simplest recipe ever.

SERVES 4

800g/1lb 12oz boned lamb, cubed (loin chops are good – but expensive; leg is standard for kebabs, but our Kashmiri butcher uses shoulder, which, with sufficient marinating, is an excellent and tasty choice)

3 tbsp olive oil

1½ level tsp salt

1 tsp coarsely ground black pepper

TO SERVE:

4 tomatoes

flatbread

lemon wedges

Put the meat into a bowl, add the oil and seasoning, mix well, before covering the bowl and chilling for 8–24 hours. Remove the meat from the fridge around 20 minutes before you need it: fridge-cold meat often burns on the outside before the inside is cooked.

When you are ready to cook, light the barbecue or preheat the grill. Thread the cubes on to skewers and cook over hot coals or under the hot grill, turning regularly: the meat will need about 6–7 minutes altogether. Halve the tomatoes and thread these on to skewers to cook alongside the lamb.*

Serve the *chenjeh* kebabs with the tomatoes in warm flatbread, accompanied by plenty of lemon wedges and perhaps a herby onion salad.

*Tip on cooking
Everything cooks at different speeds, so tempting though it is to alternate meat and vegetables on one skewer to make it look pretty, it is nearly always best policy to do things the Iranian way and cook the different ingredients of a barbecue separately.

BALUCHI *CHAPLI* KEBABS

FEEDS 4–6 WARRIORS

750g/1lb 10oz minced (ground)
   lamb (traditionally mutton)
3 tbsp roasted chickpea (gram)
   flour
2 tbsp crushed coriander seeds
2 tbsp crushed anardaneh
   (see p.58; or use 1 level tbsp
   sumac, or the grated zest of 2
   lemons)
2 tsp ground cumin
3–4 green chillies, chopped
   (or use 1 tsp chilli powder)
1 bunch of spring onions
   (scallions), very very
   finely chopped
½ bunch of fresh mint, chopped
½ bunch of fresh coriander (cilantro), chopped
1 egg
3 large tomatoes, cut into
   thick slices
oil, for frying

TO SERVE:

hot flatbreads
raw onion rings
chopped raw chilli (optional,
   of course)
lemon wedges

Baluchistan – such a lovely name for a nation, but very few people know where or what it is. I only know a bit about it because quite a lot of Baluch seem to live in South London. It is, like Kurdistan, a country without borders, a confederation of Kureishi Arabs (in all likelihood from Syria) and Iranian tribes occupying southeast Iran, southern Afghanistan and southwestern Pakistan. In Iran and Pakistan, there are provinces named accordingly, but there is a strong core of Baluch who would like to see their country attain independence.

The Baluch culture is colourful: clothing, music and literature are full of character. And the cuisine is a delightful mix of the subtlety of Persian and Arabic cuisine with the full-on spices of the lands to the East.

This is one of those lovely recipes that come with a spurious story attached; the fifteenth-century legend of Sheh Murid. It is the tale of a tragic love triangle between the noble and skilful young warrior Sheh Murid, his childhood sweetheart Hani and his friend, Mir Chakar. As the result of a rashly made pledge, Sheh Murid was honour-bound to give Mir Chakar the hand of Hani. To avoid the torture of seeing his woman at the side of another man, Sheh Murid took himself into exile and became an ascetic, devoting himself to God. Despite a potentially promising twist in the tale, Sheh Murid eventually chose God over Hani and rode off into the sunset on a white camel, never to be seen again. Sheh Murid is hallowed as a minor saint in Baluchistan.

It is rumoured that *chapli kebab* was created in the image of the great hero's shield; others say that it represents the sandals that he used in his wanderings as a holy man (*chapli* means 'flat shoe' in Pashto). Whatever the origins of the dish, it remains popular street fare across the region.

Mix all the ingredients (up to and including the egg) for the kebabs together and chill for an hour or so to enable the flavours to mingle.

When you are ready to cook, form the meat into around 12 balls, then flatten and shape them into, well, shield shapes. Press a slice of tomato into the meat one side. Heat some oil in a pan and fry the patties both sides until golden, taking particular care when cooking them with the tomato side down.

Serve immediately with bread, raw onion, chopped chilli and lemon, and perhaps some yogurt to take care of the heat.

OLIVES WITH WINGS

Versatile though chicken is, it is truly one of my least favourite comestible items. But wings I can always manage. Gotta love chicken wings. It's like the Great Food Designer (assuming one goes with the theory that we are meant to eat meat: but here is not the place to get into that debate) gave us the chicken as meal food, and then added the wings in case we felt like snacking later. They are perfect snack fare – one or two bites and they're gone – and they're so responsive to marination.

I first tried 'barbied' olives in Greece – and was very pleasantly surprised. The charcoal adds a real smokiness to them.

MUNCHIES FOR 4

FOR THE CHICKEN:
8 chicken wings, skin on
1 tbsp Turkish black olive paste (or tapenade)
2–3 garlic cloves, minced
½ tsp ground black pepper
1 level tsp dried rosemary
juice and zest of ½ a lemon

FOR THE OLIVES:
around 24 large green olives, pitted
the other ½ of the lemon,
    cut into quarter slices
1 tbsp olive oil
½ tsp dried thyme
2 garlic cloves, minced

Put the chicken in a bowl. Mix all the other ingredients for the chicken together and spoon it over the chicken using your hands to work the marinade into the meat. Cover and set aside for around 30 minutes (out of the fridge will be fine as long as it is only 30 minutes).

Same with the olives: pop them in a bowl and add all the other ingredients.

When you are ready to cook, light the barbecue or preheat the grill. Thread the wings on to skewers and grill for around 3 minutes per side, or until cooked. While they are cooking, wrap the olives (plus marinade) in a foil parcel and pop it over the cooler end of the barbecue (or in the oven if you're doing stuff indoors).

Serve hot as a barbecue starter or leave in the fridge as a very moreish any-time snack.

AFGHAN *SHAMI KABOB*

A while back, an unusually chubby young Afghan came to do a couple of days' work for us. He rejoiced in the rather splendid forename of Gul-Agha, which means Mr. Flower (this isn't strictly necessary for you to know in order to make kebabs, but it has always made me smile). Anyway, we realised that he wasn't the ideal long-term staff solution that we had been seeking as he looked set to eat his way through all the profits: he never stopped snacking. *Shami kabob* is apparently his favourite fare, and as he remains a good customer, he was happy to elicit and share this recipe from his sister's mother-in-law's neighbour's granny (or some such). There is a shortcut version at the bottom of the recipe.

This isn't really meat-on-sticks, as *shami kabobs* are actually fried. But this very fact makes them easy to make at home. Always make extra as they are perfect to keep in the fridge for grazing teens or abnormally peckish staff.

Put the split peas into a pan with the lamb and onion. Add the potatoes to the pan together with the cinnamon, cardamom, cloves, ginger, garlic, chilli and just enough water to cover. Bring to the boil, then turn down the heat and simmer for around 1 hour, or until the split peas and the lamb are truly tender.

Drain the mixture, retaining the stock, and fish out the cinnamon sticks. Either mince the meat, vegetables and remaining spices together, or place it all in the blender along with the egg, cumin and coriander and salt (if you go for the mincing option, then clearly you should add the egg afterwards). If you are blending the meat, be careful not to over-process it or it will become quite gloopy and unworkable. If the mixture seems too dry, add a little of the reserved stock; if it is too wet, a spoonful of flour usually does the trick.

Chill the 'kabob' for 30 minutes–1 hour: this will make it easier to shape. When you are ready to cook, use wet hands to shape the mince into 9–10cm/3½–4in long sausages (the traditional shape: there is of course nothing stopping you making them any shape or size you like). Heat a little oil in a frying pan and cook the kabobs in batches until they are golden brown before scooping them out on to kitchen paper to drain.

Serve wrapped in bread with plenty of fresh herbs, some zinging chutney, raw onion and lemon wedges.

MAKES ABOUT 12

100g/2⅓oz/½ cup yellow split peas (preferably chana dal)

500g/1lb 2oz lamb (preferably shoulder), boneless and cut into small pieces*

1 onion, quartered

1–2 medium potatoes (around 150g/5½oz worth), peeled and chopped

2 cinnamon sticks

2–3 cardamom pods, pricked

2–3 cloves

2cm/¾in knob fresh ginger, peeled and roughly chopped

3–4 garlic cloves, roughly chopped

1 hot green chilli, destalked

1 egg

1 tsp ground cumin

1 tsp ground coriander

1 tsp salt

* In a hurry?
Just use minced (ground) lamb mixed with cooked split peas, boiled mashed potato, grated onion, diced garlic, ginger and chilli. And use pre-ground versions of the spices.

QUAIL ON STICKS

FEEDS 6 AS A STARTER
OR SNACK

1 tsp fennel seeds

2 tsp coriander seeds

1 tsp cumin seeds

3 tsp *anardaneh* (sun-dried
     wild pomegranate seeds,
     optional)*

3 garlic cloves

1 tsp ground ginger

1 tsp ground cinnamon

½ tsp ground chilli

3 tsp sea salt

4 tbsp olive oil

6 nice plump fresh quail

Little birds. To the ancients they must have seemed like a limitless source of snack-shaped gifts from Mother Nature. Easy to catch, cook and eat. Arriving in migratory fashion quite often at precisely the time when other food became scarce. To be fair, they were widely enjoyed in Europe until comparatively recently (remember the four and twenty blackbirds baked in a pie?), and the French were ever partial to brandy-soaked ortolan. But something happened along the historical way, at least in northern Europe: we got conservation-conscious, aware of threatened species, and at the same time the need to catch our own food was removed. Little birds became 'cute'. Taboo as food. And many of them became protected.

But across the Middle East, no such taboos exist: still to this day songbirds of all shapes and varieties are caught, quite often cruelly, and consumed. The trade in small birds is especially reprehensible in Cyprus, where the dish of ambelopoulia is much prized: the birds (mostly blackcaps) are often caught in glue traps. Elsewhere methods are less cruel, but the practice is no less common-place: in Iran, my in-laws talk of buying bags of (net-caught) assorted little birds from the bazaar to marinate and barbecue – they find my RSPB membership and slightly daffy relationship with our local starlings unfathomable.

Anyway, rather than give you a recipe for barbecued bulbul or snack-sized sparrow burgers, here's perhaps a more acceptable one for an easy quail kebab.

Quails somehow have escaped the taboo (sadly this may be because they don't sing and they're not that pretty): they are farmed, readily available in our supermarkets, and 'enjoying' renewed popularity on the British dinner table. They are also hugely popular across the Middle East, from simple supper grills to elaborately stuffed banquet fare. Claudia Roden writes of quail flying south and dropping from exhaustion on beaches in Alexandria, whereupon happy locals would gather them up and gobble them up. Recipes for them abound all the way from Morocco to Afghanistan.

* Anardaneh
(sun-dried wild
pomegranate seeds)
These seeds add a nice tartness
to dishes. They are available
in Middle Eastern and Indian
shops, but they can be hard to
find, so you can leave it out
of this recipe or substitute
2 teaspoons ground sumac
(which you should then add
at the same stage as the chilli).

Toast the fennel, coriander, cumin and *anardaneh*, if using, in a wee frying pan until they start hissing at you. Tip them into a pestle and mortar or spice grinder (hey – an old tea towel will do) and pound them. Next add the garlic, ginger, cinnamon, chilli and sea salt and work the ingredients into a paste, trickling the olive oil in slowly.

Now rinse the quail and pat them dry. Butterfly them by cutting along the backbone, opening them out and flattening them with the palm of your hand. Rub the flavoured oil all over the birds, cover and chill for a few hours.

When you are ready to cook, light the barbecue or preheat the grill. Thread each flattened quail on to 2 skewers (threaded about 4cm/1½in apart) and grill them over hot charcoal – 3–4 minutes a side should do the trick. Alternatively, cook them under the hot grill until done. Serve with flatbread and plenty of lemon wedges: a tomato and onion salad on the side would be nice 'n' all.

Gyros
THE PORK AND CHIPS BUTTY

MAKES ABOUT 10

FOR THE *GYROS*:

1kg/2lb 4oz pork taken from
the eye of the shoulder
(AKA pork neck fillet/
tenderloin, a tender yet
flavoursomely fatty cut)

100ml/3½fl oz/scant ½ cup
red wine vinegar

50ml/1¾fl oz/scant ¼ cup
olive oil

5 garlic cloves, minced

1 tbsp dried oregano

1 tbsp paprika

1 tsp ground cumin

1 tsp cracked coriander seeds

1½ tsp crushed sea salt

1½ tsp crushed black pepper

FOR THE CHIPS:

10 potatoes, peeled and cut into
thin chips (keep them in water
if you are prepping ahead)

olive oil, for frying

TO ASSEMBLE:

250ml/9fl oz/generous 1 cup
thick plain yogurt

1½ tbsp English mustard

2 tsp dried dill

salt and freshly ground
black pepper

10 slices of pitta (try to get the
special round ones if you can)

4–5 firm tomatoes, thinly sliced

1 large white onion, thinly sliced

The sandwich that makes the doner look like health food. Well maybe that's a slight exaggeration – but this is one chin-dribbling, fatty, cholesterol-laden, glorious snack. The perfect street food munch for when you've had one too many ouzos up the *bouzouki* bar – or when you're having an informal get-together at home. Many of you will have tried *gyros* in Greece: it is *souvlakia*'s fast food cousin. Beguilingly aromatic sizzled pork is crammed into a circular pitta pocket with a hefty chip garnish. *Opa!*

Notwithstanding the fact that few domestic kitchens actually have a vertical grill, it is quite possible to make a jolly decent *gyros* approximation at home. Napkins at the ready?

Using a very sharp knife, cut the pork into thin slices, less than 1cm/½in in thickness, then cut each slice into teensy striplets, around 4cm/1½in in length. Bash the meat with the palm of your hand and set it aside.

Beat all of the other ingredients for the gyros together in a bowl before adding the meat and turning it over so that it is thoroughly coated. Tip it into a (hole-free) plastic bag, tie the bag loosely at the top and pop into the fridge. It needs a good 2 hours – overnight would be better still – during which time turn the meat over in the marinade just by manipulating the bag.

Mix the yogurt, mustard and dill together with just a dash of seasoning and chill until needed.

When you are ready to cook, preheat the oven to 200°C/400°F/Gas mark 6. Shallow-fry the potatoes in batches in olive oil and pop them in a tray in the bottom of the oven to keep warm. While you are doing this, drain the meat, tip it into an oven tray and slide it in to cook. It will need only about 15 minutes, so keep an eye on it.

Once the chips are ready and the meat is crispy-cooked, grill or bake the pitta bread until it starts to puff up, then make an incision along the side of each piece to form a pocket. Spoon a little of the yogurt sauce into each, along with a few slices of tomato and onion. Use tongs to distribute the meat between the pittas, and dollop a handful of chips artfully into each. Now get your guests to form an orderly queue...

Handy knife hint #1: The gentle art of tomato cutting is made considerably easier/safer if you use a bread/serrated knife. The serrations grip and penetrate the fruit rather than sliding off or squashing it.

Handy knife hint #2: Blunt knives are so much more dangerous than sharp ones: sharp knives will cut with precision; blunt ones are more likely to slide or bounce off the object you are cutting and 'collide' with your finger. But you all knew that, right?

THE HOME *SHAWARMA* EXPERIENCE

Shawarma, the ultimate test for a wannabe vegetarian. Don't eat a lot of meat myself: in fact I could easily give it up tomorrow. Except... except... Oh the greasy-chinned, garlic-sauced, slightly chilled joy of a hot *shawarma kebab* on a cold autumn evening: that is one carnivorous pleasure I could never entirely renounce.

Of all the kebabs in this chapter, this is the one dish which I can't help feeling might be best left as street food, but it is pretty easy to re-create at home. The word *shawarma* is derived from the Turkish verb 'to turn', but in truth you don't need an upright spit: this method just needs a griddle or frying pan. And you could always walk up and down in the road outside your house chomping the thing if you really want your *shawarma* experience to feel totally authentic.

Note: this needs 24 hours' marination.

MAKES AROUND 6,
WITH LEFTOVERS FOR LUNCH
THE NEXT DAY

FOR THE MARINADE:
1kg/2lb 4oz boned leg of lamb (or use
    the equivalent weight of bone'd
    chicken – roughly 2 boned birds)
6 garlic cloves, minced
2 tsp ground cinnamon
2 tsp ground allspice
1 tsp ground cardamom
1 tsp ground cumin
½ tsp ground cloves
½ tsp ground nutmeg
1 tsp salt
½ tsp ground mastic (optional)*
250g/9oz/generous 1 cup plain yogurt
    (inauthentic, but for the
    home-experience, yogurt seems
    to bring out a stronger flavour)

3 tbsp apple vinegar
2 tbsp olive oil

FOR THE GARLIC SAUCE
(AKA THOOM):
1 whole bulb garlic, peeled
big handful of chopped fresh parsley
1 tbsp lemon juice
pinch of salt
200–250ml/7–9fl oz/¾–generous 1 cup
    olive oil

TO ASSEMBLE:
3 large *khobez* (Arabic flatbreads,
    like huge pitta bread)
Iranian or Arabic pickled cucumbers
    (i.e. spicy ones, not sweet)
Kebab Salad Mix
    (see bonus recipe opposite)
chilli sauce (optional)

* Mastic

This is funny, chewy, resiny stuff. Gets used in such a worrying range of industries that one is left wondering about its suitability as a foodstuff. It appears mostly in sweet recipes these days, but in Middle Eastern kitchens of yore it was used as an aromatic spice in savoury dishes and is mentioned extensively in Al-Baghdadi's thirteenth-century cookery book. It is widely available in Middle Eastern and Greek shops, but you can just leave it out of this recipe: its effect is subtle. To use, take one or two granules and crush them to a powder; you can then use it as you would any other spice.

Cut the lamb (or chicken) into narrow striplets, 6–7cm/2½–2¾in in length and just 1–2cm/½–¾in in width. Discard any really tough gristle, but leave all the fat on the meat. Mix the garlic and the spices into the yogurt along with the vinegar and oil, stir well before adding the meat and mixing thoroughly. Cover and chill for 24 hours.

Next for the *thoom*. This is much easier with a blender. Lob in the peeled garlic, parsley, lemon juice and salt. Blend well, then very slowly trickle in the olive oil: we are making an emulsion and if you rush it, it will crack/curdle. If you want the sauce thicker, add more olive oil: if it turns out too thick, whisk in some more lemon juice or water. Pour it into a bowl, cover and chill.

When you are ready to cook, heat your griddle plate (or barbecue) or frying pan and sizzle off the marinated meat in batches: each batch should take just 2–3 minutes, but if you are using chicken, make sure it is cooked through. Pop the cooked meat into a warm oven to keep hot until you are ready to wrap and roll.

Warm the *khobez* just a little, then split each piece into 2 discs. Place 1 disc on a board in front of you, then stripe some pickled cues and kebab salad across its width, just short of the middle, i.e. so that two-thirds of the bread is visible above it and the other third is peeking out on the side nearest your tummy. Spread some of the cooked meat over the wrap, then spoon some of the *thoom* and chilli sauce, if using, over it. Now roll the bread up, starting at the shorter end. Once you have rolled as far as the filling, use your little fingers to tuck in the excess bread flaps so that the filling is completely encased in bread. Roll it right up, wrap it in a twist of paper, then repeat with the other discs of bread. Enjoy...

BONUS RECIPE: KEBAB SALAD MIX

This is so useful for barbecues: in fact, it will go with just about any hot sandwich, and when I worked at a kebab joint we got through about 10kg of this stuff each opening session. Just mix very finely sliced white cabbage with very finely sliced onion. Add some very finely sliced tomato and cucumber halves (i.e. cut into semi-circular slices) and lots of chopped herbs of your choice (mint, parsley and coriander/cilantro are the obvious ones). Add salt and pepper and dress with lemon juice as desired.

BONUS RECIPE: GLUTEN-FREE FLATBREAD

A handy hint for those of you whose relationship with wheat has gone sour. You can still enjoy barbecues with flatbread: just make your own. It is very simple: I got this recipe from the lovely Pippa Kendrick in two tweets, thus:

Sally Butcher @PersiainPeckham
@friendlyfood Hiya! You got any good (easy) recipes for gluten-free flatbread?

Pippa Kendrick @friendlyfood
@PersiainPeckham I do! 110g of gluten-free flour (or 55g gram flour & 55g of gluten-free flour) ¼ tsp xanthan gum (essential), salt, 1 tbsp oil, 4–6 tbsp warm water

@PersiainPeckham sift, pour over oil & water and pull together into smooth dough. Griddle them over high heat for 3 mins each side. Makes 2

RABBIT AND FIG KEBABS

SERVES 4

FOR THE RABBIT:

1 nice (albeit headless) rabbit,
    skinned and jointed*

1 tbsp red wine vinegar

2 tbsp date syrup (if you cannot
    find any, use honey instead)

2 tsp harissa paste

4 garlic cloves, minced

2 tsp dried thyme

1 heaped tsp ground cumin

1 tsp ground coriander

1 tbsp rapeseed (canola) or
    sunflower oil

1 level tsp salt

FOR THE FIGS:

8 small fresh figs (yes, you can
    used canned ones if they
    are out of season)

150g/5½oz/⅔ cup *labneh* or
    cream cheese

½ tsp ground cumin

handful of fresh mint, washed
    and shredded

oil

* Rabbit

You can use boned rabbit, but
there is a kind of Neanderthal
appeal in eating any barbecued
meat on the bone.

Rabbit is widely enjoyed around the Mediterranean and across North Africa, but it does not feature so much in the cuisine further East. That is not to say that it is not eaten East of Ankara: the rabbit must have seemed like a wild snack back in the day, readily available in the wildest and remotest landscapes, easy to catch and relatively easy to clean and cook. And it is still consumed across Iran, Iraq, Afghanistan and all the other -istans. But it is not regarded as a delicacy, and when talking to customers from those parts, they often dismiss it as 'peasant fare'. Furthermore, some Muslims question whether it is halal or not.

I first enjoyed sizzling, aromatic rabbit kebabs at a midsummer fiesta on a sweltering Manchegan night: I have to confess that this recipe is born of that somewhat seminal experience, but the flavouring owes a bit to Morocco and another bit to Turkey. The dates and figs give this quite a festive feel: perfect fare for a Hallowe'en or Guy Fawkes barbecue perhaps...

First catch your rabbit... or pay a trip to your butcher. Wash the rabbit joints and pat them dry. Mix all the other ingredients together in a bowl, and add the bunny, turning it over so that it is well coated. If you have time, chill for 6 hours, or overnight: if time is limited, score through the flesh on the thicker joints of meat, tip it into a plastic bag with the sauce, and leave it somewhere 'ambient' for 30 minutes, or so.

Remove the stalky bit from the figs with a pointy knife, and use a teaspoon to excavate a little of the fig flesh (which you may eat: cook's pickings and all that). Mix the cream cheese with the cumin and the mint, and spoon it into the fig cavities. Next brush the outside of the figs with a little oil, and nestle them into foil, either as a parcel or individually.

When you're ready, light the coals on the barbecue (or heat the grill/oven – the latter should be set at 190°C/375°F/Gas mark 5). Rabbit joints take slightly different times to cook, so arrange the coal so that it is hotter at one end. Remove the meat from the marinade (which you should reserve for basting) and shake it to remove any surplus liquid. Skewers aren't essential, although the use thereof does make turning the meat over easier. Generally speaking, the further towards the rear of the rabbit from which a joint comes, the longer it takes to cook: thus you need to put the rear legs kind of over the coals, the saddle (AKA middle bit) next to them, and the front legs furthest away from the heat. Thus arranged, the meat should take around 8 minutes per side to cook through: use the reserved marinade to brush on the rabbit if it starts to look dry. If you are cooking in the oven, the rabbit should take about 40 minutes: put the rear legs and saddle in first, and the front legs after 10 minutes.

Pop the figgy foil parcel/s on to the grill and cook for around 6 minutes or until the cheese is piping hot (they will take slightly longer to cook in the oven).

Serve the rabbit and figs with a crisp green salad and some warm flatbread.

AUBERGINE-WRAPPED CHICKEN

MAKES 12

FOR THE MARINADE:

3 plump chicken breasts,
    skinned and off the bone
3 tbsp plain yogurt
4 garlic cloves, minced
juice and zest of 1 lemon
1–2 tbsp olive oil
1 level tsp ground turmeric
2 tsp Aleppo pepper
    (or substitute 2 tsp paprika
    with a pinch of chilli flakes/
    red pepper flakes)
½ tsp salt

TO ASSEMBLE:

2 large aubergines (eggplants)
salt
oil
125g/4½oz/1¼ cups grated
    kashkaval cheese (OK –
    Cheddar will do)
handful of fresh mint, shredded
cocktail sticks (or bamboo
    skewers, presoaked
    and halved)
400ml/14fl oz/1¾ cups tomato
    passata (strained tomatoes)
    or juice

This is a quintessentially Turkish dish, as it comprises the two ingredients without which no Turkish chef can cook: yogurt and aubergine.

I saw something like this on sale in a bustling takeaway in the touristy part of Turkey, but as we had two petulant teens in tow I was not allowed to stop and indulge. This is my effort to re-create the dish back home, although I will now of course just have to imagine the softly lapping Mediterranean, the moon rising across the bay, the smell of herbs and kebabs hovering over the port and the gentle sound of bickering stepchildren.

Lay each chicken breast flat, then slice through them horizontally so that you end up with 4 very thin slices from each one (a nice butcher might do this for you). Beat the yogurt with all the other marinade ingredients, then immerse the chicken in the mixture. Chill for at least 2 hours; 6–8 would be better.

When you are ready-ish to cook, slice the aubergines thinly lengthways: again you need 12 slices. Rub each slice with salt and leave pressed between some sheets of kitchen paper for around 20 minutes. At the end of this time, wipe the aubergines dry, then fry them in hot oil just until they are soft and floppy. Drain them on more kitchen paper and allow them to cool just a little.

Preheat the oven to 200°C/400°F/Gas mark 6.

Place a slice of aubergine in front of you and sprinkle it with grated cheese and a sprinkle of mint. Remove a chicken slice gently from the marinade and layer it on top of the aubergine, then roll the whole thing up into a sausage. Secure the bundle with a cocktail stick and repeat with the rest of the slices. Place the aubergine rolls in an ovenproof dish, and pour the passata around them. Bake uncovered for 15 minutes; then cover with foil and cook for a further 15 minutes.

Serve the parcels with a diced tomato, onion and cucumber salad (or the Salata Duco, see p.121), some yogurt and hot pitta bread. And don't forget to remove the cocktail sticks before tucking in.

Meat Not On Sticks

MOTHER-IN-LAW'S *TAS KEBAB*

COMFORT FOOD
FOR 4–6

2 onions, sliced

1 leek, roughly chopped

3 sticks of celery, cut into
　fat chunks

1 chicken, skinned and cut into
　8 pieces

1 tsp ground turmeric

1 tsp lime powder

salt and freshly ground
　black pepper

2 carrots, cut into fat sticks

1 green (bell) pepper, cut
　into chunks

6–8 mushrooms, wiped

½ small butternut squash, peeled
　and cut into chunks

3 medium waxy potatoes, peeled
　and cut into slabs

1 large aubergine (eggplant),
　cut into 2cm/¾ in cubes

200g/7oz/1 cup prunes (soaked
　if necessary)

2 tbsp good tomato paste

1 can (400g/14oz) chopped
　tomatoes

around 1 glass water

1 tbsp olive oil, for cooking

Tas kebab is one of those funny recipes that rumbles around the kitchens of the Middle East with no one quite knowing whence it came. It is a popular and homely dish in countries from Bulgaria all the way round to the Levant, with a small detour to Iran. Even the name is a puzzle: *tas kebab* is a juicy baked meat dish bearing little resemblance to the doner kebabs we know and love/despise.

Every country/province/village/household makes it differently, but the principles are the same: meat or chicken is layered with vegetables and fruit and baked in a fragrant tomato sauce. In Turkey, *tas* means bowl, and *tas kebab* is usually prepared contained within an inverted bowl in the oven: the Persian version we offer here is much simpler. Unlike most of the *khoreshts* (stews) of Iran, *tas kebab* is usually eaten with bread as a comforting supper: the leftovers make for great any-time snack food. It is hearty fare, but economical, as the ingredients are varied according to season and market price. I usually make it with the leftover pieces of vegetables in the bottom of the fridge. It is lovely with cooking apples or quince when they are available. My mother-in-law normally uses chicken (as here), but occasionally she will prepare it with baby lamb *kufteh*.

My, this is easy. But we might have mentioned that already. Preheat the oven to 190°C/375°F/Gas mark 5.

Layer the onions, leek and celery into the bottom of a fairly deep baking tray. Arrange the chicken on top and sprinkle it with the spices and seasoning. Dot the rest of the vegetables and the prunes evenly around and on top of the chicken.

Mix the tomato paste, tomatoes and olive oil together, and add the cold water. Pour the liquid over the chicken and vegetables, cover the tray properly with foil and bake for around 1 hour 10 minutes, or until the chicken is cooked through and the vegetables are tender. Serve with warm bread.

Dizzee

MASHED LAMB WITH STOCK

This isn't quite street food, but it is served at transport caffs up and down Iran: it is the favourite fare of Persian lorry drivers. It is also probably Iran's favourite comfort food. I once tried to serve this to guests, and my mother-in-law looked at me with as much horror as if I had been dishing up dinner in my PJs: this is schlepping around the house food, not posh food.

Dizzee was historically (and may still be) a way of stretching a few meagre bones into a nourishing meal. The idea is that lamb is bubbled away with potatoes and beans and (usually) dried limes until it literally falls off the bone. The meat is stripped from the bone and mashed up with the pots/beans (using a special meat tenderiser known as a *gusht coup*), while the stock (and the bones: the lamb marrow is one of the best bits, and if you don't want it, save it for me) is served alongside in a mini tureen called a *dizzee* (whence the dish gets its name).

The stock, which is known as *ab gusht* ('meat-water'), can be eaten as a soup; it should also be mentioned that the meat is sometimes left in the stock and relished as an accompaniment to rice.

Place the lamb in a pan with the chopped onions and dried limes. If you are using dried beans, rinse and add them now. Cover with water so that the surface of the liquid is about 5cm/2in above the meat (only 2cm/¾in if you are using canned beans), sprinkle in the turmeric and bring to the boil. At this stage, you may want to skim the surface of the water: both the beans and the lamb are prone to producing scum/foam. Turn down the heat and simmer the *ab gusht* for around 1½ hours.

After this time, lower the potatoes in; if you are using canned beans, add these now together with the tomato paste. Check that the meat is still covered by the stock (add a little boiling water to top it up if necessary), and only now should you add some seasoning to taste. Cook for another 30 minutes, or until the potatoes are just starting to disintegrate.

Drain the *ab gusht* through a sieve, retaining every last drop of that lovely stock. Using a fork, pull the meat away from the bones and return any of the bones that are likely to contain marrow to the stock. The dried limes can be discarded at this stage, although hardcore Iranians would probably eat them.

Ideally you should give each person a little bowl of stock, a pile of the cooked lamb/beans/potatoes, and a *gusht coup* so they can mince it themselves. In practice you may want to pound the lamb yourself (so that it is mashed, not puréed), and dish it up family style, with the stock in a separate bowl. *Dizzee* needs lots of warm bread to accompany it: I also rather like frying off some cubed stale bread and floating it into the *ab gusht*. Serve with pickles, yogurt and raw onion wedges.

SERVES 8

1 shoulder of lamb, trimmed and chopped on the bone into 4cm/1½ in cubes
2 medium onions, chopped
8–10 dried limes, pricked
100g/3½ oz/½ cup chickpeas, soaked overnight (or use 1 can/400g/14oz)
100g/3½ oz/½ cup butter (lima) beans (or cannellini), soaked overnight (or use 1 can/400g/14oz)
2 tsp ground turmeric
4 medium potatoes, peeled and cut in half
1 heaped tbsp tomato paste
salt and freshly ground black pepper

Halim

A RAMADAN/STREET BREAKFAST

SERVES 6–8 PEOPLE
AT LEAST

500g/1lb 2oz/scant 2⅓ cups
    pot barley
1 medium skinned chicken
1 tsp ground turmeric
½ tsp salt (or so)
butter
ground cinnamon
sugar

Meat porridge. Hmm. This at first seems to be quite the weirdest dish. But it is utterly delicious, and combines a double whammy of comforting carbohydrate with the culinary hug that chicken soup gives you.

Halim is in fact made across most of the Middle East: in Pakistan, it is a spicy dish made with puréed beef, while in Armenia it is a paste which is eaten with bread. In Arabic countries, it is more often known as *harisseh* (which just means 'well-cooked'). I offer you the Persian version as it is the simplest.

In Iran, it is eaten as a hearty breakfast (it is in fact so satisfying that it is also great for lunch or supper), especially in the bazaars of the land, and is most popular during Ramadan. While it is made at home, it is first and foremost street food: children are often sent out to *halim* vendors with empty bowls at the crack of dawn to fetch enough to feed the family. Three points to note: firstly, most Iranians make this dish with wheat instead of barley, but in truth they are largely interchangeable; secondly, they would always use hulled grain, but as most of the goodness is in the husk, we prefer to leave it on; thirdly, the dish is also nice (and more traditional) with lamb or turkey.

Soak the barley for 3–4 hours.

Place the chicken in a large pan, cover with plenty of water, add the turmeric and salt and boil for around 1 hour. Strain off the stock and trim all the flesh from the chicken.

Put the barley in the pan together with the water in which it has been soaking, add the strained chicken stock and the flaked chicken. Bring to the boil, then turn down the heat and simmer for at least 2 hours (in Iran, they would get up before dawn to get this dish underway, but if you are having it as breakfast we recommend making it the day before). Check it at regular intervals – you may need to add a drop of boiling water if the liquid content is insufficient. The barley is cooked when it is soft and gloopy. When you are happy that this is the case, take off the heat and add more salt to taste. Now comes the fun part – traditionally you would pound this in a pestle and mortar, but to be perfectly honest we just chuck it all in the blender. Return the gloop to the pan (it should have a slightly reluctant pouring consistency) and warm through.

To serve, melt some butter (around 40g/1½oz/3 tablespoons per bowlful) in a saucepan and let it simmer until it starts to darken and hiss. Ladle the *halim* into bowls and drizzle a little butter on top of each; sprinkle each with cinnamon and 2 teaspoons sugar. If you are not eating it all at one sitting, it will keep in the fridge for around four days; just make sure that you sizzle your butter freshly every time.

CHICKEN LIVER WITH POMEGRANATE SAUCE

OK, so I thought my husband had flipped when he came up with this little 'snackeroony' one evening. Turns out that it's the speciality at one of the (Syrian) restaurants which we supply, and the chef had made a bit extra for him one evening. Jamshid liked it so much he rushed home and made it for me.

It is the perfect fare for those not too fond of the peculiarly earthy flavour of liver: used in moderation, pomegranate paste works as an agent to mask strong odours and tastes in food. Of course, if you use too much you can kill a dish at 20 paces.

SERVES 4 AS A *MEZE* DISH
OR 1 HUNGRY HUSBAND
olive oil, for cooking
2 garlic cloves, minced
250g/9oz fresh chicken livers (preferably
    organic or those sourced from
    free-range birds)

1 hot green chilli, or to taste
2–3 tbsp pomegranate molasses
pinch of sea salt
generous handful of fresh parsley,
    chopped
khobez flatbread, to serve
squeeze of lemon, to serve

Heat the oil in a pan, toss in the garlic and after a few seconds add the chicken livers and chilli. Stir constantly for a few moments more before stirring in the pomegranate molasses and adding a little salt to taste. The chicken livers should be just cooked/slightly pink in the middle: overcook them and they will taste like a grubby eraser. Take off the heat and cover with the chopped parsley.

To serve, heat the *khobez* through, slide it onto a plate and pile the liver on top. Add a squeeze of lemon and the dish ends up with a perfect balance of sweet and sour and umami and salt and bitter (really – it has everything).

Andreas' Sheftalia
CAUL-WRAPPED MEATBALLS

I've been making these moist and moreish meatballs for years, but to get the perfect, authentic lowdown I sent my brave, self-sacrificing husband out to play *takhte-nar/tavoli*/backgammon and drink coffee with our Cypriot Ealing Massive connections. Quite a few hours later, he came back with sheets of scribbled notes and a furrowed brow: the Cypriots do like a good debate, especially when food is involved. Sisters and mothers had been consulted, and there had been a lot of hand-waving.

The recipe is a hybrid via Alkis and Andreas. Andreas has been in catering all his life and knows pretty much everything there is to know about snacking, especially meat snacking. He is the only man I know who can turn a plate of discarded cooked chicken bones and a scrap of bread into a feast fit for Olympus.

The traditional way to make *sheftalia* would involve 200g/7oz each pork and lamb mince, plus 100g/3½oz chopped pork fat, but most housewives these days just use fatty minced pork.

TO FEED 4

500g/1lb 2oz coarsely ground pork mince
(neck end is best: it needs to be fatty)
1 large onion, finely chopped
1 bunch fresh parsley (including stalks),
chopped

⅓ tsp each salt and freshly ground
black pepper
1 tsp ground cinnamon
100g/3½oz banna or pork caul
(posh name = omentum)

Preheat the barbecue.

Mix all the ingredients bar the caul fat together, pounding well with your hands so that the fat starts to soften.

Stretch the caul fat out, marvelling at its weird texture, then cut it into 16 x 5–6cm/ 2–2½in squares. Take a small lump of the meat mixture, roll it into a small fat sausage shape and place it in the middle of one of the caul squares. Pull the caul fat up around the meat – the stuff is conveniently self-sealing – and repeat with the rest of the mixture.

Sheftalia only really works on charcoal, as the caul fat comes into its own when exposed to direct heat, basting and sealing in the flavour as it melts: cook for 20 minutes, turning them often. You can cook them indoors if it really isn't barbecue weather: poach them in boiling water for around 10 minutes, then pop them into a really hot oven pre-heated to 220°C/425°F/Gas mark 7 (or under a really hot grill) for another 10 minutes.

Serve with bread and loads and loads of lemon wedges.

Chorba Frik

ALGERIAN STREET SOUP

This is a bit like the Moroccan *harira*, but with meat. Simple-but-filling, spicy soups like this are especially popular during Ramadan and are common street fare during that month. The word *chorba* just means soup, and is used in differently spelled incarnations all the way from Kyrgyzstan to the Maghreb.

Freekeh is green smoked wheat: it is available in good Middle Eastern stores, but you can easily substitute barley, which takes about the same time to cook.

SERVES 6

100g/3½ oz/½ cup dried chickpeas
 (or use 1 can/400g/14oz)
1 large onion, diced
splash of oil, for frying
350g/12oz finely diced lean lamb
2 sticks of celery, finely chopped
1 carrot, grated
2–3 garlic cloves (although this is often
 avoided during Ramadan itself as it
 a) makes you thirsty, and b) is deemed
 disrespectful to smell of food during
 the month of fasting)

1 tsp ground cinnamon
½ tsp ground black pepper
½ tsp ground turmeric
1.5 litres/2½ pints/6½ cups water
1 tbsp tomato paste
125g/4½ oz *freekeh*
6 tomatoes, skinned and chopped
 (or use 1 can/400g/14oz)
1 small bunch of fresh coriander (cilantro),
 chopped
salt

Soak the chickpeas overnight (or at least for 6 hours), then drain.

Fry the onion in some oil, then add the lamb and celery, stirring well. When the lamb is sealed all over and the celery has begun to soften, add the carrot, garlic and spices together with the drained chickpeas (if using dried); after a few minutes more, pour in the cold water, bring to the boil, then turn down the heat and simmer for about 1¼ hours, or until the meat and pulses are just cooked.

Next, add the tomato paste, *freekeh* and chopped tomatoes (together with the chickpeas if using canned) and return to a gentle boil, adding a little more water if the *chorba* looks too thick. Cook for another 30 minutes, or until the wheat is tender. Stir in the coriander, add salt to taste and serve immediately.

Kufteh Tabrizi
POSH-ISH STUFFED MEATBALLS

There is a town called Tabriz in Iran which is renowned for crafting *kufteh*. Their most famous recipe contains a whole poussin. This recipe is slightly less ostentatious, and undeniably far more piquant and intriguing.

MEZE FOR 8

FOR THE STOCK:

1 large onion, chopped

oil, for frying

½ very hot red chilli (or 2 green chillies), chopped (optional)

1 red (bell) pepper, finely chopped

1 tsp ground turmeric

1 tbsp tomato paste

1 can (400g/14oz) chopped tomatoes

200ml/7fl oz/ ¾ cup sour grape juice (or just add extra stock and the juice of 2 lemons)

2 litres/3½ pints/8 cups good chicken stock

salt and freshly ground black pepper

FOR THE CASING:

100g/3½oz/½ cup yellow split peas (chana dal)

100g/3½oz/½ cup short-grain rice

750g/1lb 10oz minced (ground) lamb

1 large onion, grated

1 tsp ground turmeric

1 tsp dried oregano

1 tsp dried tarragon

1 level tsp salt

½ tsp ground black pepper

FOR THE STUFFING:

100g/3½ oz barberries, soaked (or cranberries)

75g/2¾oz prunes, soaked and pitted

75g/2¾oz/scant ½ cup dried apricots or peaches, soaked

75g/2¾oz/¾cup walnuts, roughly chopped

75g/2¾oz/generous ⅓ cup butter

75g/2¾oz/½ cup nibbed nuts (almonds and pistachios)

50g/1¾ oz sour or morello cherries, pitted

150g/5½oz/scant 1⅓ cups breadcrumbs

1 tsp ground cinnamon

½ tsp ground cardamom

1 tbsp tomato paste

First the stock: you'll need a large pan. Fry the onion in a little oil. After a minute or so, add the chilli and red pepper, followed after a few minutes by the turmeric, tomato paste and chopped tomatoes, sour grape juice and stock. Bring to the boil, season, cover and set aside.

Next, the casing. Cook the split peas in boiling water until soft, around 35 minutes, and do the same for the rice, around 15 minutes. Drain both and cool before adding to the minced lamb along with the onion, turmeric, herbs and seasoning. Pound the mixture well: you can actually start it off in a blender unless you are up for the exercise. Chill until ready.

Finally, the stuffing. Drain the soaked fruit and pat it dry. Roughly chop the prunes and apricots/peaches. Melt the butter, and fry all the fruit and nuts together, stirring well, for 6–7 minutes. Add the remaining ingredients, cook a little more, then take off the heat.

To cook the *kufteh*, return the stock to the boil. Use wet hands to form the meat mixture into 8 large balls. Form a hollow in each one, and divide the stuffing mixture between them, closing the casing up over the filling. Drop the meatballs into the bubbling stock, cover the pan and cook for 1 hour, or until the *kufteh* have risen to the top of the stock. Serve covered with the tomato stock as hot *meze* – or cool and offer them up as a very refined picnic dish.

AFI'S LAMB ROULADE

INFORMAL SUPPER
FOR 4–6

FOR THE CASING:

1kg/2lb 4oz minced (ground)
    lamb
1 large onion, grated
½ tsp ground cumin
1 tsp ground cinnamon
1 tsp ground turmeric
1 egg
2 tbsp breadcrumbs
salt and freshly ground
    black pepper

FOR THE FILLINGS:

8 baby carrots, scrubbed,
    topped and tailed
4 eggs
1 bunch of fresh coriander (cilan-
    tro), chopped
AND
1 big bunch of spinach
100g/3½ oz/1 cup walnut
    halves, crumbled
125g/4oz pitted dried sour
    cherries or prunes

FOR COOKING:

flour (Afi uses chickpea flour,
    but plain/all-purpose flour
    will do)
splash of oil
2 tbsp tomato paste
1 tbsp lemon juice
400ml/14fl oz/1¾ cups
    chicken stock or water

Afi is my mother-in-law. She's over 70 now, but looks a good 20 years younger, and rules her little Peckham/Persian roost with tenacity, generosity, humour and a rod of iron. We get on famously, and in this I am very lucky, because Iranian mothers-in-law are notoriously pernickety, worthy of every mother-in-law joke in the book and worse.

Afi has been cooking this dish for many years and has made it quite her own, but I think it was originally based on a recipe by Roza Montazemi and the name indicates French origins (Iran has a history of trading with the French dating back to the sixteenth-century Safavid empire). It is one of the few dishes that my father-in-law will agree to eat without a mountain of rice on the side: it's usually enjoyed with bread, yogurt and fresh herbs.

Preheat the oven to 200°C/400°F/Gas mark 6.

Firstly, mix the lamb and all the other casing ingredients together, working the meat to blend all the flavours.

For the first filling, boil the carrots whole so that they are a bit more than *al dente*. Hard-boil the eggs (10 minutes with a splash of vinegar works for me) and peel them. Take half the roulade mixture and form it into 2 fat sausages. Split them lengthways and arrange the whole carrots, whole eggs and chopped herbs in the cavity thus created so that every bite and slice will look pretty. Mould the meat back to cover the hidden filling.

For the second filling, steam or stir-fry the spinach for just a few seconds. Take the rest of the minced mixture and, again, make it into 2 fat sausages, this time filling it with spinach, walnuts and fruit.

Roll each of the mince sausages gently in flour, then fry them in a little oil just to seal them. Next place the lightly browned roulades in an oven tray tin. Blend the tomato paste with the lemon juice and stock and pour it over the roulades: they should be half covered with sauce.

Cover the dish with foil and bake for 45–50 minutes. Slice thickly and serve. And there you go: Persian meatloaf – a perfect midweek supper.

Dolmeh-ye-Aloo Siah
LAMB-STUFFED PRUNES

Prunes are so often used in stuffing for meat and vegetables that it is rather nice to see them get their own back by being the main feature in this dish.

Stuffing is a big thing in the Middle East, with anything and everything from vine leaves to carp being filled with an astonishing and creative selection of pastes and pilafs. Sometimes one vegetable is filled with different stuffings, sometimes a range of vegetables are all filled with the same stuffing. Sweet, sour, rice-based, wheat-based, crunchy, soft – it's a whole sub-genre of cooking.

If you want to play, you could make up a bit more of the stuffing recipe below and bake off a range of fruit *dolmeh*: dates, peaches, nectarines, apples, plums and persimmons would all respond well. Just a thought: I'm not actually trying to create more work for you or anything.

MEZE FOR 4–5
OR CANAPÉS FOR 20

FOR THE STUFFING:
1 tbsp raisins
1 small onion, finely chopped
splash of oil
1cm/½ in piece fresh ginger, peeled
    and chopped
200g/7oz minced (ground) lamb
½ tsp ground turmeric
1 level tsp ground cinnamon

1 tsp dried mint
salt and freshly ground black pepper
1 can (400g/14oz) chopped tomatoes
1 tbsp pine nuts (or use nibbed almonds
    or pistachios)
big handful fresh parsley, chopped

TO ASSEMBLE:
20 fat, juicy, pitted prunes
1 tbsp honey
1 tbsp vinegar
big handful fresh mint, shredded

Preheat the oven to 180°C/350°F/Gas mark 4.

Soak the raisins in a little cold water. Next, fry the onion in a splash of oil. When it softens, add the ginger and the lamb, mixing well. Once the lamb has started to colour, add the spices, mint and some seasoning along with quarter of the can of tomatoes. Simmer for a few minutes, stirring constantly, then add the pine nuts, drained raisins and parsley and take off the heat.

Spread the prunes out in a small baking tray, and use a teaspoon to insert a spoonful of the mince mixture into each one. Whisk the rest of the canned tomatoes together with the honey and vinegar, and pour this 'sauce' into the base of the baking tray. Cover the dish with foil and bake for 30 minutes. Remove from the oven and sprinkle with the shredded mint. These *dolmeh* are best enjoyed hot or at room temperature, and will keep for 2–3 days in the fridge.

CHICKEN JELLY

Aspic Schmaspic. And I don't do gelatine either (it just won't dissolve for me, and clumps petulantly at the bottom of whatever I cook). But this easy, economical little recipe is a summer snacker's delight, and makes for an intriguing yet elegant *meze* dish.

I have a theory that many people don't buy chicken with much forethought. Obviously free-range birds are better all round, but I am talking basic home economics here. Regardless of the cut that you need for a particular dish, it is always more cost-efficient to buy a whole chicken (even if you don't have a stockpot constantly bubbling on your Aga), and good butchers will cut it/bone it for you as required. The point being that this recipe is a good way to use any leftover bits of the bird in question.

It is based on something my wonderfully eccentric grandmother used to make. She had an abnormal fascination with 'things in jelly': of course, as a child I really didn't want to know what lay beneath, but as an adult I have come to realise that she was an extraordinarily good cook. There is an added pinch of Claudia Roden for good measure.

A FUNKY LITTLE *MEZE*
FOR 4–6
1 small chicken (or leftover joints)
1 small onion, chopped
1 stick of celery, chopped
1 level tsp ground turmeric

salt and freshly ground black pepper
4 dried limes (or 1 small lemon, quartered)
1 tbsp dried dill
⅓ tsp ground saffron dissolved in a splash
    of boiling water
big handful of fresh parsley, finely chopped

Put the chicken in a pan with the onion, celery, turmeric, salt and pepper, adding enough water to three-quarters-cover the bird. Bring to the boil, then prick the dried limes and drop them into the pan along with the dill. Turn down the heat and simmer for about 1½ hours, keeping an eye on the liquid levels (which should be allowed to reduce by about half) and turning the chicken over from time to time. When the chicken is visibly falling off the bone, check the seasoning of the stock and take the pan off the heat.

Strain the stock into a bowl and whisk in the saffron and chopped parsley. When the meat is cool enough to handle, strip the skin off the chicken and discard. Pull the meat from the bones and arrange it in a serving dish; then pour the cooling stock over the chicken and cover. Chill overnight, during which time it will set to become a wibbly-wobbly chicken salad. If you don't like the look of the fatty bits on the surface, they can be dabbed off with a piece of kitchen paper.

Serve with pickles and a robust brown bread.

Zalatina

BRAWN

This is another of Granny Jojo's secret recipes, but with added Cypriot touches. *Zalatina* is widely enjoyed as a snack/*meze* in Cyprus, and it is a great little number to have in the fridge for summer picnicking. Jojo used to make loads and then distribute it all round the family/bridge club: obviously if you have a squeamish family or don't play bridge, just cut down the quantities accordingly.

In Cyprus, the dish was originally made by country folk as a waste-not-want-not way of using up all parts of a slaughtered pig. You can in theory use all manner of pig parts, but I have suggested ingredients that will be more readily available.

MAKES ABOUT 1KG/2LB 4OZ

1 pig head, or 4 trotters/pig's feet
    (or a combination of both)
500g/1lb 2oz neck end of pork, cut into cubes
2 leeks, chopped
2 sticks of celery, chopped (optional)
3–4 cinnamon sticks
2 bay leaves
6–7 black peppercorns
2–3 tsp salt

250ml/9fl oz/generous 1 cup white wine
    vinegar
250ml/9fl oz/generous 1 cup lemon juice

TO GARNISH (OPTIONAL):

sliced olives
gherkins, sliced
radishes, thinly sliced
fresh parsley sprigs

Righty ho, the pig's head. Get your butcher to remove the ears and shave as much of the hair from the head as possible. When you get home, wash the head thoroughly: pay special attention to sluicing out the nostrils. If you are using trotters, get the butcher to remove any hair (or do it yourself: burning it off with a match or lighter is the easiest option).

Place the head/trotters in a large pan and cover with water. Bring to the boil, turn down the heat and simmer for 10 minutes, then drain before placing the meat back in the pan. Cover with fresh water, adding the neck end of pork, leeks, celery, spices, herbs and peppercorns and salt. Return to the boil, turn down the heat and simmer for about 3 hours.

At the end of this time, strain the cooking stock into a fresh pan. Add the vinegar and lemon juice and bubble so that the amount of liquid reduces by half. Set the stock aside to cool: meanwhile, pick all the meat off the bones and cut into roughly equal-sized pieces.

You will need 2 regular-sized (500g/1lb 2oz) meatloaf tins, or the equivalent in Pyrex-type dishes. Arrange a pretty pattern of garnishy bits in the bottom of each, then pour a little of the cooled stock over them. Chill until set, then arrange the meat carefully on top, topping up with as much of the stock as it takes to cover the meat. Put the *zalatina* back in the fridge to set: once it is quite firm, you can use a hot palette knife to ease it out of the moulds and turn it out so that the garnish is uppermost. Serve in thick slices with plenty of bread and pickles or lemon.

Lahana Dolma

TURKISH STUFFED CABBAGE LEAVES
WITH BONUS GREEK SAUCE

MAKES AROUND 24

1 medium green or white cabbage
(about 1.5kg/3lb 5oz)

400g/14oz minced (ground)
lamb

100g/3½ oz/½ cup long-grain
rice (I use basmati)

1 onion, very finely chopped

2 tbsp raisins, soaked for
20 minutes and drained

2 tbsp pine nuts or sunflower
seed kernels

big handful of fresh parsley,
chopped

1 tbsp dried dill

salt and freshly ground
black pepper

slosh of olive oil

2 tbsp grape *pekmez** (optional)

FOR THE SAUCE**:

1½ tsp cornflour (cornstarch)

2 eggs, separated

juice of 1 lemon

* Pekmez

A concentrated fruit syrup,
usually made from grape or
mulberry. Available from good
Turkish and Greek shops.

** Handy hint

This classic *avgolemono* (egg
and lemon sauce) can be used
with all sorts of things, from
asparagus to fish to meatballs.

Most Middle Eastern countries stuff things, and all lay claim to inventing the idea/making the best *dolma*. Thanks to the Ottoman kitchens, the Turks field an impressive array of filled vegetables, and when it comes to cabbage leaves, they are most certainly in the lead. But in the interests of international relations, I have added some Greek sauce to the matter.

Discard any mangy looking outer leaves from the cabbage, and carefully remove and wash the rest of the leaves, one by one. Bring a large pan of salted water to the boil and blanch the leaves in batches for around 2 minutes (for green cabbage) or 3½ minutes (for white) before draining them in a colander.

Mix the minced lamb with the rice, onion, raisins, pine nuts, herbs and seasoning. Take a dessertspoon of the stuffing and place it at the stalk end of one of the cabbage leaves. Next, roll the cabbage leaf away from you, over the stuffing, tucking in the bits at the side as you go: you should end up with a small sausage shape, with the rice/meat mix completely enclosed. Repeat with the rest of the mixture, keeping any damaged leaves to one side. Place an upturned plate in the base of a saucepan, and cover it with those reject leaves before arranging the rolled dolmeh concentrically in the pan and adding the olive oil and *pekmez*, if using. Place another plate on top of the cabbage leaves, then fill the pan with water so that the leaves are just covered. Bring to the boil, cover, turn down the heat and simmer gently for about 1 hour, then take off the heat.

Remove the lid of the pan to let some of the steam out, then carefully tip the pan over a small saucepan, pressing the plate on top down to keep the *dolmeh* in place, so that any remaining cooking stock trickles out. Keep the *dolmeh* warm while you make the egg and lemon sauce.

Make the *dolmeh* stock up to around 200ml/7fl oz/generous ¾ cup by adding boiling water if necessary, then pour a little of it into a wee bowl, adding the cornflour and mixing well. Add a little more stock, stir and pour all of the cornflour mix back into the pan with the rest of the stock in it. Whisk the egg whites until stiff-ish, then beat in the egg yolks and lemon juice, followed, a little at a time, by the stock. Pour all of it back into the pan and heat gently for a few minutes, without boiling.

Arrange the *lahana dolma* on a plate, drizzle the sauce over the top, and serve hot or warm.

COOKING WITH LEFTOVERS

Of course, some of the most satisfying snacks comprise leftovers: they sate both one's hunger and one's wallet. This is a double posting of two of our favourite things to do with the rest of the Sunday roast. I have been vague about quantities, because, frankly, I have no idea how much meat you have left over. These are both chuck-it-in-the-dish-and-be-gone-with-measuring-type recipes.

SHREDDED LAMB WITH CROÛTONS

There are folks who reckon that the best thing about roast lamb is its by-products: dripping, shepherd's pie, bone marrow… Know what, I'm drooling as I type this. I am not that partial to meat, and avoided lamb altogether until I became exposed to the Middle Eastern treatment, but now there are nights when nothing else will do.

Fry 2 of the garlic cloves in plenty of oil before adding the bread cubes, stirring well, followed by the thyme. Cook for 2 minutes, then drain on a piece of kitchen paper.

Heat a little more oil in the pan and fry the onion. When it starts to colour, add the rest of the garlic together with the lamb and fenugreek and cook for 2–3 minutes. Season, add the lemon juice and simmer for a few minutes more before stirring the green stuff through the dish. Toss the croûtons on top and serve.

SERVES 2–4

5 garlic cloves, minced
non-extra-virgin olive oil
a few slices of stale bread, cut
    into 1cm/½ in cubes
1 tsp dried thyme
1 small onion, chopped
1–2 cups of leftover cooked
    lamb, shredded
1–2 tsp dried fenugreek leaves
salt and ground black pepper
1–2 tbsp lemon juice
big handful/s of fresh green stuff:
    spinach, chives, coriander
    (cilantro), parsley, watercress

CHICKEN WITH OKRA

You shouldn't really need pointers as to what to do with leftover chicken: it is one of the most versatile foodstuffs in the world. But here's our piastre's worth anyway.

Fry the onion in a little oil. Once it softens, add the garlic, stirring well, followed by the okra. When the latter start to brown, add the chicken and tomatoes, followed by the lime juice and pickle. Cover the pan and simmer for 7–8 minutes before seasoning to taste (you may not need much salt), sprinkling with chopped herbs and serving with warm bread.

SERVES 2–4

1 medium onion, chopped
oil, for frying
2–3 garlic cloves, chopped
500g/1lb 2oz baby okra (ladies'
    fingers), washed and dried
1–2 cups of leftover cooked
    chicken, cut into chunks
300g/10½ oz cherry tomatoes
juice of 1 lime
2 tbsp mango pickle
salt to taste
big handful of fresh coriander
    (cilantro) and/or mint,
    washed and chopped

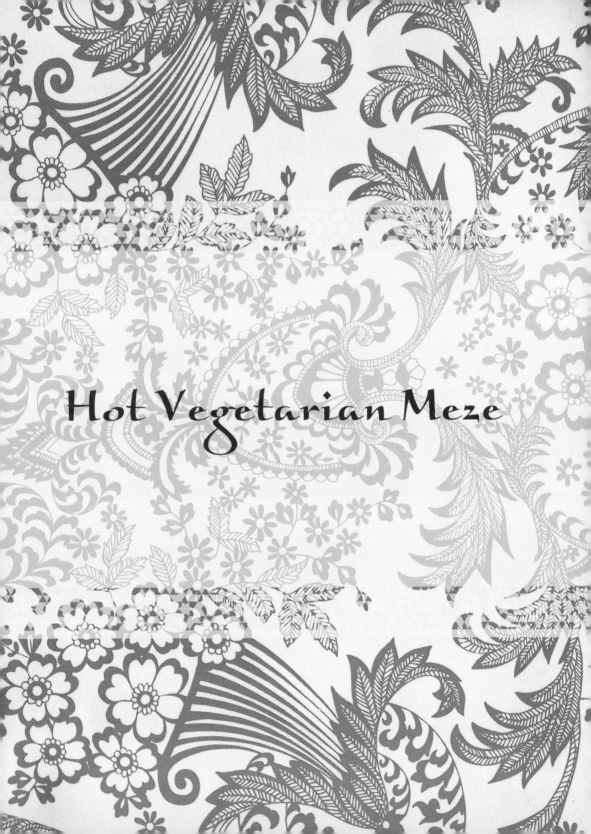

Hot Vegetarian Meze

IRANIAN STREET VEG

The heart of most Iranian towns is the bazaar – some, like Tehran and Isfahan, are truly vast, dense and often mysterious rambling mazes, a town within a town. And it is here that there is the greatest need for street food – simple snacks to nourish weary shoppers or fortify traders. Street snacks in Iran are nothing if not simple, but it is this very simplicity that intrigues me, and I have learned that they treat ingredients with great respect. Favourites in the winter months are boiled turnips or beetroot; a perennial feature are the hot potato vendors, in the spring there are broad beans, and in the summer you can buy grilled corn. Of course, such food never tastes as good as it does when eaten *in situ*, whether it be in the bitter cold or sweltering heat, out of newspaper or greaseproof cones, but I have tried to re-create some of these simple pleasures...

SHALGAM – TURNIPS

If possible, buy young, baby turnips – big old wrinklies belong to the stockpot or stew. Scrub the skins of each turnip well, then quarter them. Although the skins are not eaten, leaving them on during cooking ensures that the vegetables remain intact. Place in a pan, cover with water and bring to the boil. Do not salt the water, as this makes the turnips tough and they will take longer to cook. Turn down the heat and simmer for around 45 minutes, or until a fork prods into them with ease. Drain and serve with salt and pepper. They are absolutely delicious. But if you're still not convinced, try mashing them with a little butter and a grating of nutmeg. Or you could check out the Iraqi recipe on p.100.

LABOO – BEETROOT

To cook beetroot bazaari-style, just peel and cut them into manageable chunks. Cover with water (again, no salt), bring to the boil, then turn down the heat and simmer for 1½ hours. Convention will have you add around 2 teaspoons sugar per 1kg/2 lb 4oz of beetroot – this is a matter of taste, and I find most people make them too sweet. Just enjoy with a fork. It's not remotely authentic, but I like them with a big dollop of mascarpone on the side.

STREET CORN

Again, a very simple idea. As someone who grew up eating sweetcorn smothered in butter, this method of preparation came as something of a revelation. Grill your corn cobs whole over fire, skin them, then plunge into hot salted water for a few moments. Eat. Told you it was simple. I never thought that I would find butter superfluous to my requirements...

BOGOLI – BROAD BEANS

For *bazaari bogoli* (4 people can easily eat 2–3kg/4lb 8oz–6lb 8oz of whole broad/fava beans – by the time they are shelled they don't go very far), bring a large pan of water to the boil (again, no salt until later) and plunge them into the boiling water. Turn down the heat and simmer for around 45 minutes to 1 hour. Drain and serve still in their pods accompanied by salt, a pot of *golpar* (see p.10) and lemon wedges. Iranians invariably shuck their beans; personally, I prefer to eat them with the skin on.

BABY AUBERGINE *DOLMEH*

This is a recipe from our chiller cabinet. It's really kind of Mother Nature to design stuff in snack-sized portions as well as its regular size. Baby aubergines are perfect for snacking on, and these *dolmeh* (which are kind of like mini *Imam Biyaldi*) make a wonderful meze dish.

You can use white or purple varieties: the white ones are usually chunkier and need a bit more cooking – although having said that, they are often eaten raw and are not unpleasant *al dente*.

MAKES 8

8 baby aubergines (eggplants)
salt
1 small red onion, roughly sliced
2 garlic cloves, sliced
16 shelled walnut quarters

8 pitted dates, halved
1½ tbsp grape *pekmez*
   (or pomegranate molasses)
4 tbsp tomato concasse (or juice)
½ tsp chilli (red pepper) flakes
1 tbsp olive oil

Make a lengthways incision in each of the aubergines, taking care not to pierce right through. Sprinkle a little salt into each of the cavities, and rub it in before inverting the vegetables onto kitchen paper to drain for 30 minutes.

Preheat the oven to 190°C/375°F/Gas mark 5.

Wipe the aubergines to remove any residual bitterness/water/salt. Insert a chunk of onion and a couple of slices of garlic into each cavity, then press a couple of pieces of walnut and date into each. Layer them into an ovenproof dish.

Whisk all of the other ingredients together and drizzle the resulting sauce over the aubergines. Cover the dish and bake for around 40 minutes, or until the aubergine flesh is soft when you poke it.

Enjoy while still warm: these make a great meze item, or a posh addition to your picnic.

Kabak Kizartmasi

TURKISH COURGETTE FRITTERS WITH YOGURT 'SAUCE'

You can practically coat anything in batter and fry it and you will get a queue of salivating people at your kitchen door. Obviously this is not everyday food (because we are all watching our fat intake, yes?), but it is a simple snack option and makes for a great little *meze* dish.

The Turks seem partial to vegetables thus prepared and there is a whole range of *kizartmasi* dishes: aubergines, carrots, cauliflower and potato all get the same treatment. But courgettes, with their refined bitterness, lend themselves particularly well to the creamy crunchiness of batter.

MEZE FOR 4

150g/5½ oz/generous 1 cup plain
    (all-purpose) flour
½ tsp salt
½ tsp ground black pepper
125ml/4fl oz/½ cup beer (yes, you may drink
    the rest of the can: be a shame to waste it)
1 level tsp ground turmeric
1 level tsp paprika
2 large courgettes (zucchini), cut into
    3–4mm/⅛–⅙ in slices
oil, for frying

TO SERVE:

100g/3½ oz/scant ½ cup plain, not too
    thick yogurt
4 garlic cloves, minced
pinch of salt
drizzle of olive oil
squeeze of lemon
Aleppo pepper (or a mix of cayenne
    and paprika)

Sift 100g/3½oz/scant ¾ cup of the flour into a bowl along with the salt and pepper, then slowly whisk in the beer until you get a smooth thick batter. Set the bowl aside for about 1 hour so that the batter can 'rest'.

Scatter the rest of the flour on a plate and mix in the turmeric and paprika. Dip the courgette slices in and out of the flour. Heat a good slug of oil in a frying pan and give the rested beer batter a good stir. Take one of the floured courgette slices and dunk it into the batter; allow to drain, then fry in the hot oil, turning after 2 minutes, until it is golden on both sides. Repeat with the rest of the courgettes: you will probably have to cook them in two batches.

Mix the yogurt with the garlic, adding salt, olive oil and lemon to taste. Sprinkle the *kizartmasi* with the Aleppo pepper, and serve them on a plate with the garlic sauce in a bowl on the side.

THREE-PEA 'TAGINE'

As tagines go, this is a doddle, and it is so easy on the eye as practically all the ingredients are spherical. It is a quick dish to prepare, and so if you are lucky enough to own a tagine dish, you can either use it as a serving dish, or transfer all the ingredients into your tagine at the same time as you add the green peas: pop it in the oven at 150°C/300°F/Gas mark 2 for around 30 minutes, or until you want to serve.

The addition of warm 'dunky' bread makes it a great informal supper dish, or you could cook less and dish it up as part of a *meze* spread.

MOROCCAN TV SUPPER FOR 4

400g/14oz can chickpeas, drained
  (or 100g/3½ oz/½ cup dried chickpeas,
  soaked overnight)
200g/7oz/1 cup chana dal (split yellow peas)
75g/2¾ oz/½ cup raisins
1 large onion, chopped
olive oil, for frying
3 garlic cloves, minced
1 level tsp ground ginger
1 tsp ground turmeric
1 level tsp ground cumin
1 tsp ground cinnamon
½ tsp chilli (red pepper) flakes (optional)
550ml/18fl oz/scant 2½ cups vegetable stock
  (or water)
350g/12oz/3 cups frozen peas (or fresh if it is
  that time of year)
around 12 cherry tomatoes
salt and freshly ground black pepper
½ bunch of fresh coriander (cilantro),
  chopped
½ bunch of fresh mint, shredded

If you are using dried chickpeas, rinse them and cook in fresh water for about 1½ hours, or until they are soft without falling apart: the addition of a pinch of bicarbonate of soda will accelerate the cooking process.

Soak the chana dal for around 45 minutes. Likewise, the raisins, although they only need 20 minutes' soaking time.

Fry the onion in a little oil, then once it has softened and become translucent, add the garlic and spices and cook for 2 minutes, stirring constantly. Add the stock or water and bring to the boil before lowering in the drained chana dal, turning the heat down and leaving to simmer (you may need to top up the cooking liquid during this time).

After about 45 minutes, drain the raisins and add them to the tagine together with the cooked chickpeas, frozen peas, cherry tomatoes and a little salt and pepper. Bubble away for a further 10 minutes, or until the peas and tomatoes are cooked. Take the pan/tagine pot off the heat or out of the oven, check and adjust the seasoning, and finally sprinkle the contents liberally with the chopped herbs. Enjoy hot or just warm.

Perfect for a Sunday evening in front of the TV, watching *Casablanca* of course.

Esfanaj va Rivas
SPINACH WITH RHUBARB
AND POMEGRANATE

I frequently put together something like this for my lunch. It is a well-known fact that shopkeepers are tied to their tills on very long pieces of elastic, and always have to be 'back in five minutes'. Stir-fries like this are therefore a boon: they take little more than five minutes to prepare, and are certainly healthier than going down the fish and chip shop.

This recipe is based on one of my favourite Persian *khoreshts* or casseroles: the original dish comprises chicken, which I don't really like and which clearly takes a little longer to cook.

SNACK LUNCH FOR
1 HUNGRY SHOPKEEPER
2–3 spring onions (scallions), chopped
sunflower (or other) oil, for cooking
½ tsp ground turmeric
1 garlic clove, chopped
big handful of parsley, roughly chopped
big handful of mint, roughly chopped
1 glass water (about 150ml/5fl oz/⅔ cup)
½ can (200g/7oz) chickpeas, drained
2–3 sticks of rhubarb, peeled if large, mature
    stalks and cut into 3cm/1¼in chunks

1 tsp sugar
½ bunch of spinach, roughly shredded
juice of ½ a lemon
1 tbsp pomegranate molasses (or *pekmez*, see
    note on p.80, or just add extra lemon)
salt and freshly ground black pepper
    and sugar if required
fresh pomegranate, to garnish (optional:
    pomegranates are a winter fruit, while
    rhubarb is at its best in early summer)

Fry the onions in a splash of oil. Once they have softened, add the turmeric and garlic followed by the herbs. Cook for about 5 minutes, stirring well, before adding the water. Bring the contents of the pan to the boil, then add the chickpeas, rhubarb and sugar. Simmer for around 5 minutes before adding the spinach, lemon juice and pomegranate molasses. Bubble for 5 minutes more, season to taste and serve with warm bread. Scowl at the customers knocking on the door and indicate that they should form an orderly queue until you have finished your lunch...

This combo is famously 'cold' (*sard*) in Persian dietetics – only the mint and the chickpeas are 'warm' (*garm*). Iranians to this day believe that you are what you eat, and that all food has hot or cold properties which serve to slow down or accelerate your metabolism. Too much cold food leaves you feeling bilious and out of sorts; too much hot food can leave you restless and febrile. By way of example, alcohol is very 'cold', which is why so many hangover cures comprise 'hot' (stodgy, greasy) foods. So now you know.

Qorma-e-Piaz

AFGHAN SWEET-AND-SOUR ONION HOTPOT

* Ajwain seeds

These are also known as carom seeds or bishop's weed. They are highly aromatic and used mostly as a home remedy in Afghanistan: they are chewed to sweeten the breath, and made into a decoction for all manner of digestive ills. In food they are used sparingly: the flavour is somewhere between aniseed and thyme, but very strong. In most recipes, they can be replaced by cumin seeds.

* * Pine nuts (jalghouz)

These are big (in size) in Afghanistan and very popular. They are most frequently enjoyed roasted in their skins, in much the same way as pistachios. Most Middle Eastern recipes involving pine nuts have their origins in the Levant and Turkey: they get into *kibbeh*, puddings, rice, stuffing… There are two problems with them: one is that they are fiendishly expensive. The other is that the Chinese variety can cause a nasty reaction known as Pine Mouth: it is harmless but deeply unpleasant, as it results in everything tasting metallic or bitter for days (for more about this, see veggiestan.com). Pumpkin and sunflower seed kernels make admirable alternatives, and are both a lot cheaper and healthier.

This is an unusual recipe. I've always thought that it takes a brave cook to create a dish without onions in it: turns out it feels just as weird placing the onions centre stage. *Qorma* is a generic Afghan term used for food cooked in a sauce which has been thickened with vegetables or pulses or nuts – in other words, a fat, satisfying, pleasingly oily stew.

SIMPLE SUPPER FOR 4

100g/3½ oz/½ cup chana dal (split yellow peas)
75g/2¾ oz/½ cup raisins
oil, for frying
½ tsp ajwain (or use caraway seeds)*
1 tsp mustard seeds
2 garlic cloves, minced
1 large onion, diced
1 red (bell) pepper, diced

2 green chillies, chopped
1cm/½ in stub fresh ginger
½ tsp ground turmeric
1 tsp garam masala
around 20 (small) shallots, peeled but left whole
2 tsp tomato paste
2 tbsp vinegar
salt, to taste
50g/1¾ oz/generous ⅓ cup pine nuts**

Pick through the the chana dal and soak them in cold water for around 45 minutes. The raisins also need soaking, for about 15 minutes.

Heat a good slug of oil in a decent-sized (and fairly deep) frying pan. Once it is sizzling hot, toss in the ajwain and mustard seeds, stirring constantly, followed by the garlic. Cook for less than a minute, then scoop them out of the oil with a slotted spoon and set aside. Once the oil is hot again, tip in the onion, pepper, chilli and ginger and cook until the onion has softened. Add the spices, followed a few moments later by the shallots. Cook until they have started to brown, and then stir in the tomato paste and vinegar.

Drain the chana dal and raisins, and add them to the pan together with just enough water to cover everything. Set to simmer: the *qorma* will need about 50 minutes to cook through. Just before you want to serve and eat, season the dish to taste before stirring the reserved fried seeds and garlic back into the pan. Finally, dry-fry the pine nuts until they start to colour.

Serve the *qorma* garnished with the toasted pine nuts; warm flatbread and some nice thick yogurt make fitting accompaniments.

LETTUCE *KOOKOO*

Kookoo (great name, no?) are basically Persian omelettes. They can be made as individual patties, or as a regular, circular, pan-sized job. And they come in a huge range of flavours, from sugary through to sour. The most famous type is *kookoo-ye-sabzi*, which is a lush herby snack, often studded with barberries and walnuts. But more recently my *kookoo* of choice has been this one. This is for several reasons: firstly, I always experience a shiver of culinary excitement when I cook with lettuce. I mean, it's a salad vegetable: cooking with it just seems so *avant garde*; secondly, it is a handy way to use up sad, soggy neglected leaves; and thirdly, it is so easy to make.

SERVES 6 AS A SNACK

3–4 spring onions (scallions), diced
oil, for frying (rapeseed/canola is a healthy
    option and is growing in popularity
    across the Middle East)
12 eggs

2 tsp plain (all-purpose) flour
¼ tsp bicarbonate of soda (baking soda)
½ medium iceberg lettuce, cross shredded
    (but not too fine)
salt and freshly ground black pepper

If lettuce feels like a Western thing

Let's face it, our salads invariably consist mostly of the stuff, whereas it seldom dominates in Middle Eastern salad bowls. It has in fact been enjoyed across the region for thousands of years, chiefly thanks to the Egyptians' discovery that eating lots of it can make you rather frisky (although, confusingly, the ancient Greeks later worked out that if you eat just a little it is quite soporific): this is because it contains stimulating tropane alkaloids (a bit like the nightshade family), but I will refrain from getting any more technical as we are meant to be cooking rather than discoursing ethnobotany.

Heat a dash of oil in a frying pan and sizzle the onions until they have softened. Take off the heat and drain on kitchen paper.

Break the eggs into a bowl and whisk well before beating in the flour and bicarbonate of soda. Add the lettuce and the cooled spring onion to the mix, together with 1 level teaspoon of salt and a healthy sprinkle of pepper.

Heat some more oil in the frying pan: you need it to be just-before-smoking hot. Using a tablespoon, dollop the eggy mixture into the oil in rough, flat oval shapes, allowing them to cook for 2 minutes before turning them over with a spatula. When the kookoo are golden brown on both sides, scoop them on to kitchen paper to drain. Repeat until you have cooked all of the mixture.

Serve hot or cold wrapped in flatbread of your choice: pickles and fresh herbs would be nice but optional extras.

Beid Baghdadi
SPECIAL BAGHDADI EGGS

When it comes to the human diet, the egg most certainly came before the chicken – we've been snacking on them practically from the moment we slithered out of the sea (or whatever). They are referred to in ancient Mesopotamian texts, represented in Egyptian hieroglyphs and much fêted by the Romans (who ate them with nearly every meal). And there are quite a few recipes for them in Al-Baghdadi's thirteenth-century oeuvre: here are two of the most user-friendly recipes from that tome (i.e., the ones that don't call for sheep tail fat, rancid barley and blood...).

BAID MUTAJJAN AKA FRIED EGGS

For when you've got that morning-after-the-epoch-before kind of feeling...

Heat a good slosh of oil in a frying pan and crack the eggs in. As they start to set, sprinkle them with the spices followed by the soy sauce. Serve with warm bread. Medieval fancy dress is optional.

MEDIEVAL BRUNCH
FOR 2–4
sesame oil, for cooking
4 large free-range eggs
¼ tsp ground cinnamon
¼ tsp ground cumin
¼ tsp ground coriander
½ tsp soy sauce

BAID MAKHSOUS AKA SPECIAL EGGS

I first came across this recipe in an art installation by the rather wonderful Jake Tilson. His culinary derring-do sent me skedaddling off to find the original *Kitab al-Tabih*: it is a recommended tome for those with an interest in Middle Eastern food history, and Charles Perry's translation is very accessible.

Heat a dash of sesame oil in a frying pan and toss in the celery and caraway seeds. Once the celery has softened, add the other spices, stirring well, then add the vinegar. Bring to the boil, season to taste and crack the eggs carefully on top. Cover the pan and fry/steam until the eggs are set. Sprinkle with paprika (an inauthentic extra) and serve (preferably from the pan – eggs are always better out of the pan) with warm bread. Share with your favourite vizier.

MEDIEVAL BRUNCH
FOR 2–4
sesame oil, for cooking
3–4 sticks of celery, chopped
½ tsp caraway seeds
¼ tsp ground cinnamon
½ tsp ground coriander
¼ tsp ground saffron dissolved
    in a splash of boiling water
4 tbsp red wine vinegar
salt and coarsely ground
    black pepper
4 large free-range eggs
paprika, to garnish

Saganaki
FLAMING CHEESE

Mmmmm. Fried cheese. Halloumi is not the only hot turophilian delight to emerge from the lands abutting the Aegean: the Greeks have a penchant for frying all sorts of cheese, and it is a hugely popular *meze* dish. The word *saganaki* refers not only to the offering of fried cheese, but also to the dish in which it is served: a small, two-handled sizzler tray, a bit like an Indian tandoor. Seafood and some vegetables can also be prepared and served in a *saganaki*.

You can just flour and fry the cheese, but this flambé version lends a little theatre to the dish – and food is always better with added theatre.

Dip the cheese slices either in water or milk and allow to drain for a few seconds before coating each slice with flour. Melt the butter in your *saganaki* dish (a frying pan is just fine), adding a glug of oil to stop the butter burning. Once it is sizzling hot, fry the coated cheese for 2 minutes per side, or until it just begins to assume an appetising golden colour.

If you are showing off, now is the time to assemble your guests. Hold the spoonful of ouzo over the pan, and touch a flame to its surface. Tip it over the cheese and shake the pan, thus eliciting 'oohs' and 'aahs' from your (apparently easily impressed) audience. Sprinkle with plenty of black pepper, garnish with the lemon wedges and serve immediately.

SNACKETTE FOR 4

8 thick (1cm/½ in at least) slices
    cheese: ideally a hard Greek
    cheese such as *kefalotyri*,
    halloumi or *kasseri*, but
    mozzarella or red Leicester
    work well too
water or milk, for dipping
flour, for coating
50g/1¾oz/3½ tbsp butter
oil, for frying (olive is best)
1 tbsp ouzo (or brandy)
freshly ground black pepper
1 lemon, cut into wedges

FRIED WATERMELON WITH HALLOUMI

We got really excited when we first realised that you can fry watermelon. It feels kind of wrong, wayward, wacky – and everyone needs to be wrong, wayward and wacky in the kitchen sometimes. Watermelon has always been a perfect foil for cheese, and no time is a bad time for halloumi, and so we thought we'd just try sizzling them together. Lo – a new snack addiction was born.

Sprinkle both sides of each slice of watermelon with the spice mix. Pour enough oil into a frying pan so as just to cover the bottom, and heat it to sizzling point. Fry the watermelon; once it is hot all the way through, remove the slices to a plate. Now fry the halloumi quickly on each side: it should be golden but not dark brown. Spread the halloumi on a platter, arrange the watermelon on top, and sprinkle the whole lot with mint. Don't burn your mouth as you scoff.

SERVES 6 AS A REAL
SIMPLE *MEZE* DISH

12–15 'triangular' slices
    (7–8mm/⅜in thick)
    of watermelon, skinned
2–3 tsp Harissa Spice Mix
    (see p.21)
olive oil, for frying
1 pack (225g/8oz) halloumi,
    cut into 12–15 slices
    (3mm/⅛in thick)
big handful of fresh mint,
    shredded

Shahan Fouls
SUDANESE MASHED BROAD BEANS

BREKKIE FOR 4

300g/10½ oz/scant 1¾ cups
    whole dried broad (fava)
    beans, soaked overnight
pinch of bicarbonate of soda
    (baking soda)
2 tbsp unroasted sesame oil
salt
1 tsp ground cumin
½ tsp ground fenugreek seeds
100g/3½ oz white (feta-style)
    cheese, crumbled
4 eggs
oil, for frying
2 large tomatoes, cut into chunks
1 small onion, cut into chunks
1 green (bell) pepper, chopped
2–3 green chillies, chopped

Sudan's culture and cuisine have a lot in common with the rest of the Middle East. And they make cracking fouls medammes: this is a popular breakfast/street dish throughout the region. You know, I could write a book just filled with fouls recipes, there are that many out there...

Cook the beans with the bicarbonate of soda in a pan of water for around 2 hours until really soft, then drain and mash them with the sesame oil, salt to taste and spices. Stir in the crumbled cheese.

Fry the eggs and serve the Shahan Fouls with the eggs on top and the chopped vegetables in separate bowls so your fellow breakfasters can help themselves. Oh, and you'll need some warm moppy bread to go alongside.

Shalgam-bi-Dibs
TURNIPS WITH DATE SYRUP

**GREAT WINTER
SNACK FOR 1**

1 tbsp butter
1 medium turnip, peeled and
    cut into thin slices, around
    2mm/¹⁄₁₆ in thick
6–8 pitted dates
2 tsp date syrup (if unavailable,
    1 tsp blackstrap molasses
    will do the job)
salt and freshly ground
    black pepper

Dates fried in butter are as close as it gets to pudding nirvana. Except this is a savoury dish. Fried dates appear as an unusual accompaniment to all manner of Middle Eastern foods, from chumming up with scrambled egg as a nutritious breakfast to garnishing some of Iran's finest rice dishes.

In this Iraqi recipe, they raise the humble turnip into something rather awesome. It also works well with parsnips, marrow and squash, and is a good way of using up the sad unloved vegetables at the bottom of your vegetable rack.

Heat the butter in a small frying pan and sauté the turnip slices for a few minutes on each side. When they start to colour, add the dates, stirring well. Cook for a few more minutes, or until the turnips are quite soft, then stir in the date syrup. Bring to the boil, season to taste and serve.

Chakchouka

TUNISIAN EGGS WITH ATTITUDE

Of recipes for scrambled eggs incorporating vegetables, herbs and spices there are aplenty, but this offering from North Africa ramps up the spice quotient and leaves the eggs perfectly poached and whole. This is perfect Sunday brunch fare – it will certainly enliven your breakfast table conversation – but it makes a good snack any time. Feel free to add some spicy chopped *merguez* sausages.

Cook the onion and pepper in a generous quantity of olive oil. When they soften, add the courgette and garlic, stirring well. After a few minutes, add the cumin and tomatoes, followed by the tomato and harissa paste. Next pour in the tomato juice, season to taste and bring the contents of the pan to a gentle simmer.

    Make 4 small 'wells' in the vegetable mixture, crack an egg into each, then cover the pan. Cook until the eggs are set, around 10 minutes, and sprinkle with parsley. Serve straight from the pan with warm bread.

SERVES 4

1 medium onion, chopped
1 green (bell) pepper, chopped
good olive oil, for cooking
1 courgette (zucchini), diced
2 garlic cloves, minced
½ tsp ground cumin
4 large tomatoes, cut into chunks
2 tsp tomato paste
2 tsp harissa paste
100ml/3½ fl oz/scant ½ cup
    tomato juice (or water)
salt to taste
4 large free-range eggs
big handful of fresh parsley,
    chopped

CARROTS COOKED IN *PEKMEZ*

Carrots are such humble, obliging vegetables: it is nice to give them their own little dish in which to star. The Moroccans make much of them in salad, but this recipe owes more to Turkey and Iran, whence the vegetable in all likelihood originated. Early, wild species of Asian carrots were magenta in colour, so these fancy-coloured jobs you see in supermarkets are in fact nothing new.

Blanch the carrots in boiling water for 2 minutes, adding the orange peel to the boiling water for the last 30 seconds. Drain the contents of the pan, reserving about 50ml/1¾fl oz/ scant ¼ cup of the water.

    Melt the butter in a frying pan and add the carrots, orange and ginger. When the carrots start to brown, tip the *pekmez* and orange blossom water into the pan along with the reserved cooking water, stirring well, then add the brown sugar. Bubble for a few minutes, season and serve sprinkled with the nibbed nuts.

MEZE OR SIDE FOR 4

500g/1lb 2oz carrots, peeled and
    cut into chunky sticks (unless
    very thin, in which case halve
    them or cook whole)
25g/1oz dried sour orange peel
    (or pare the skin from a fresh
    orange and cut it into very
    thin strips)
100g/3½ oz/7 tbsp salted butter
1cm/½ in knob fresh ginger,
    peeled and minced
50ml/1¾ fl oz/scant ¼ cup
    grape *pekmez* (or use
    pomegranate molasses)
1 tsp orange blossom water
2 tsp brown sugar
salt and ground black pepper
50g/1¾ oz/⅓ cup nibbed
    pistachios (or almonds)

Salads and Cold Meze

Borani-ye-Bademjun
AUBERGINE WITH YOGURT

**MAKES A SMALL
BOWLFUL**
2 medium aubergines (eggplants)
2 medium onions, peeled
3–4 garlic cloves, peeled
oil, for frying
1 tsp garam masala
400g/14oz/1¾ cups thick,
    plain yogurt
salt and ground black pepper

Tip
This makes a good sarnie filling
and a great meze item. It is far too
good a dish to be the preserve of
pampered royals: those naturally
inclined to snacking would be
well advised to keep a yogurt
dish in their fridge at all times.

Borani refers to a range of yogurt 'dips' named after a very spoilt queen
(and apparently inveterate snacker) called Pourandokht. Unlike *çacik/tsatsiki*
(yogurt with cucumber and mint) and *must-o-moussir* (yogurt with spring garlic),
borani dishes are made with cooked vegetables.

Preheat the oven to 190°C/375°F/Gas mark 5.

Prick the aubergines and bake for around 15 minutes, or until soft. Cool a little.

Reserving half an onion, chop the rest along with the garlic and fry them in a little oil
until the onion softens. At this stage, add the garam masala. Cook a little more before setting
these too aside to cool.

Now peel some (but not all) of the skin away from the aubergines (it's good to leave a
little on as it gives dishes a chunky homemade feel to them – I am always a little suspicious
of perfectly homogenised food). Scoop the aubergine together with the cooled onion/
garlic mix into a blender and give it all a very quick whizz (or chop through thoroughly with
a knife) before stirring the mixture into the yogurt. Season to taste.

Chop and fry the other half of the onion until it becomes quite crispy and brown, then
leave to cool. When it is cool, use it to garnish the *borani*.

Mish
PALESTINIAN CHILLI YOGURT SALAD

**MAKES A DECENT
BOWLFUL
NOTE: PREPARE 1 DAY
IN ADVANCE**
2 tsp fenugreek seeds
2 tsp chilli (red pepper) flakes
2½ tbsp olive oil
½ tsp salt
1 unwaxed lemon, washed
500g/1lb 2oz/generous 2 cups
    plain yogurt
250g/9oz/generous 1 cup *labneh*
    or cream cheese

This is a rustic Palestinian dish. Not that I know many rustic Palestinians. I made
some chillied *tsatsiki* (which I smugly thought was my own invention) in the shop
one day, and one of my customers told me about *mish*, which has been eaten in
the Middle East for centuries. There is something fun about chilli-stoked yogurt
dishes: the idea that the yogurt cools as the chilli burns as the yogurt cools...

Soak the fenugreek seeds for 36–48 hours, changing the water after the first day. Roughly
crush the chilli flakes and add them to the oil along with the salt, then set aside for 24 hours
so the flavours can mingle.

When you are ready to make the *mish*, drain the fenugreek seeds, then finely dice the
lemon, skin and all (yes, really). Beat the yogurt together with the *labneh*, then add the
fenugreek seeds, chilli oil and chopped lemon, mixing well. Cover and chill in the fridge
overnight. Enjoy with warm bread as a *meze* dip or as an accompaniment to other dishes.

It's *houmous*, Jim, but not as we know it... Well here's the thing. You cannot possibly write a book about Middle Eastern *meze* and snacking without including houmous. It is found on restaurant tables across the region, and holds all number of dishes together. Furthermore, it is a well-known fact that most of the vegetarian population of the universe actually live on the stuff, breakfast, lunch and dinner. Here is my stock recipe for it with a few variations on the theme. *Houmous*, for all you closet etymologists and pedantic Arabists out there, is actually the Arabic word for chickpeas.

BASIC *HOUMOUS BI TAHINA*

MAKES JUST ENOUGH
FOR TODAY –
SHOULD SERVE 4–6
PEOPLE

200g/7oz/scant 1¼ cups dried
    chickpeas, soaked overnight
4 tbsp tahina
2 tbsp really good extra-virgin
    olive oil
juice of 2–3 lemons
about 4 garlic cloves
salt and freshly ground
    black pepper

TO SERVE:
olive oil, for frying
paprika

The most important thing about *houmous* is that you eat it as fresh as possible. I would also advise against cheating by using canned or jarred chickpeas – they never have the same flavour. I actually like *houmous* while it is still slightly warm.

Reserve a handful of soaked chickpeas, put the rest in a pan, cover them with water and bring to the boil. Turn down the heat, allow to bubble for around 10 minutes, then skim off any foam or detritus that has risen to the top. Cook for a further hour, or until they are soft and can easily be squidged between your finger and thumb. (Chickpeas vary, and you may find that you have to cook yours for nearly 2 hours: a pinch of bicarbonate of soda will accelerate things.) Do not drain, but remove the lid and leave them somewhere for 30 minutes or so to cool a little.

You can do the next bit by hand, but it is much easier with a blender. Ladle about half of the chickpeas into a blender, including quite a bit of the chickpea cooking water. Add half of the *tahina*, olive oil, lemon juice and garlic and blend until smoothish, adding more of the cooking water if the mixture is too solid. Repeat with the rest of the ingredients, then mix the 2 batches together well and season to taste.

Heat a little olive oil in a pan and fry the reserved chickpeas, stirring constantly, until they are golden and crisp to bite. Drain them on a piece of kitchen paper then roll them in a little salt.

Serve the *houmous* on a plate/s – if you bash the bottom of the plate against the palm of your hand the dip will spread evenly across the surface. Sprinkle the fried chickpeas across the *houmous*, and follow it up with a pinch of paprika.

Serve as a dip or a sauce or a sandwich filling.

FANCY *HOUMOUS BI TAHINI*

FANCY *HOUMOUS BI TAHINI* #1
WITH POMEGRANATE AND RED PEPPERS

This is a spicy and piquant version. Make the *houmous* as opposite, but using 150g/5½oz/ scant 1 cup chickpeas and just 2 tbsp *tahina* plus 1 tbsp lemon juice. Preheat the oven to 190°C/375°F/Gas mark 5 and roast 2 red (bell) peppers for around 30 minutes, or until they are quite charred. Place them in a plastic bag for 10 minutes and you will find the skin flakes off easily. Remove the seeds and blend them into the houmous along with 2 tbsp pomegranate molasses, ¼ Scotch bonnet chilli (or other hot pepper) and 1 level tsp ground cumin. Garnish with fresh (or dried) pomegranate seeds if available.

FANCY *HOUMOUS BI TAHINI* #2
WITH TARRAGON AND OLIVES

This is an intriguing mix of umami-ness. Make your *houmous* exactly as opposite, but using just 150g/5½oz/scant 1 cup chickpeas, and adding 1 tsp dried tarragon together with 200g/7oz/scant 1¼ cups pitted green olives. Season the dip at the end, as olives are invariably salty. Be radical and garnish the dish with ... an olive.

MUSHY PEA *HOUMOUS*

Fish and chips and mushy peas, with a Middle Eastern twist.

Make pitta bread chips by heating pitta bread, splitting it, cutting it into triangles and frying it in oil spiced with coriander, cumin, garlic and chilli and draining on kitchen paper. Make fishy goujons by coating fish striplets firstly in seasoned flour, then egg and finally breadcrumbs mixed with *za'atar*. Fry until crispy golden (then either keep warm or reheat when required). And then the *pièce de résistance* – mushy pea *houmous* as a dip to go in the middle.

If using marrowfat peas, drain most but not all of the liquid away. Put all the ingredients except the oil and salt in a blender (or a big bowl if you are going to blend it all manually) and mix for 2 minutes: you are aiming for a dip with texture rather than a homogenised green paste. With the motor still running, trickle in the olive oil and season to taste. Chill for 30 minutes, or so (anything with tahina in it will thicken considerably in the fridge). Sprinkle with sumac before serving.

Arrange your cooled pitta 'chips' and hot goujons (plus a few lemon wedges) on a platter with a bowl of pea houmous in the middle. Great fun.

COMFORT SUPPER FOR 4 (A BIG BOWLFUL WITH ENOUGH LEFT OVER FOR A PACKED LUNCH THE NEXT DAY)

2 small cans (around 360g/12oz drained weight) mushy or marrowfat peas
1½ tbsp *tahina*
1½ tbsp lime juice
½ tsp ground cumin
½ tsp dried mint
½ tsp chilli (red pepper) flakes (optional)
2 garlic cloves, peeled
1–2 tbsp olive oil
salt, to taste
sumac, to garnish

Ajvar ve Pinjur
A PAIR OF DIPPY THINGS

Ajvar and *pinjur* sound like Disney penguin names, but they are actually both Eastern European/Turkish relishes, created to preserve the pick of the season so that it can be enjoyed throughout the year. They often get muddled up, and with good reason: *ajvar* is basically a red pepper paste to which some people add aubergines, while *pinjur* is an aubergine dip to which some people add red pepper. Confusing, no?

Each recipe makes enough for a big bowlful – although Middle Eastern households will make HUGE batches of this stuff and 'lay it down' for a rainy day.

They are both brilliantly snackable: keep jars of them in your fridge, and you can use them on everything from crackers to pizzas to stir-fries. Another plus point is that they both have a natural affinity with cheese. *Ajvar* and *pinjur* can also be served just as they are, with dippy bread, as part of a *meze* spread.

AJVAR: RED PEPPER SPREAD

8 red (bell) peppers
2 tbsp best extra-virgin olive oil
4 garlic cloves, chopped
2–3 fresh green chillies, chopped (optional)
3 tbsp red wine vinegar
salt, to taste

Grill or oven-bake (at 200°C/400°F/Gas mark 6) the peppers until their skin is quite charred. Allow them to cool a little then pop them in a plastic bag for about 10 minutes. This will cause them to sweat, which makes them easy to peel: you should now be able to flake away the skin with your fingers. Remove the seeds, then blend or chop the peppers – aim for chunky rather than puréed.

Heat the oil in a frying pan gently (extra-virgin olive oil has a low smoke point) and quickly fry the garlic and chillies before tipping the peppers in, followed by the vinegar. Stir well, season to taste and simmer for around 30 minutes. Allow to cool before spooning into a sterilised jar (see p.10). *Ajvar* should keep in the fridge for about two weeks. Favourite usage: dolloped on to warm French bread with some lightly melted goats' cheese.

PINJUR: AUBERGINE DIP

2 large aubergines (eggplants)
2 large tomatoes
2 garlic cloves, minced
50g/1¾ oz/½ cup shelled walnuts, roughly chopped
2 tbsp extra-virgin olive oil
juice of ½ lemon
salt, to taste
big handful fresh coriander (cilantro), chopped

Preheat the oven to 190°C/375°F/Gas mark 5. Prick the aubergines with a fork in several places and bake them on a baking tray for around 15 minutes. Next, place the tomatoes on the same baking tray and cook with the aubergines for another 20 minutes (until the aubergines are quite soft) before taking them from the oven.

When they are cool enough to handle, skin the tomatoes. Traditionally the aubergines would also be skinned, but I rather like the artisan (AKA lazy) approach and leave the skins on. Blend (briefly) or coarsely chop the vegetables together with the garlic and nuts then whisk in the olive oil and lemon juice. Season to taste, and finally stir in the chopped coriander. Like ajvar, this will keep for a week or two in the fridge. Favourite usage: spread in a pitta pocket with fried halloumi.

BEETROOT SALAD WITH CARDAMOM YOGURT DRESSING

Lady Beetroot has but to lie down on a plate to look effortlessly alluring – if she was a real woman I'd hate her. Jesting aside, you really don't need to do much to this thrifty little root to turn it into a fine snack or *meze* dish, and this salad is nothing if not simple.

MEZE PLATTER
OR STARTER FOR 6
3 medium beetroots (beets)
100ml/3½ fl oz/scant ½ cup plain, runny
    yogurt
2 tbsp olive oil
1 tbsp *sekanjebin** (optional – you could just
    use 1 fat tsp honey instead)

1 tbsp apple vinegar
1 level tsp ground cardamom
2cm/¾ in piece fresh ginger, peeled
    and minced
salt and freshly ground black pepper
handful of fresh mint, shredded

Preheat the oven to 200°C/400°F/Gas mark 6.

Top and tail the beetroots, retaining any of the prettier parts of foliage still attached, then wrap them in foil and bake for around 1½ hours, or until they are tender when prodded. Unwrap and allow to cool a little.

When the beetroots are cool enough to handle, slice into 3mm/⅛ in (ish) thick rounds and arrange on a pretty platter. You can enjoy this salad at any temperature you like: still-warm works for us.

Whisk the yogurt together with the oil, *sekanjebin*, vinegar, spices and seasoning before drizzling it artistically over the beetroot. Strew the shredded mint over it along with any retained beet tops. Try not to drool: it is very unbecoming.

*BONUS RECIPE: *SEKANJEBIN*
(IRANIAN MINT AND VINEGAR SYRUP)

350ml/12fl oz/1½ cups water
350g/12oz/1¾ cups sugar

4 tbsp white vinegar
a dozen sprigs of fresh mint, shredded

Handy hint
If, like me, you enjoy beetroot with a little too much gusto, be advised that white vinegar and cold water and bicarbonate of soda go a long way towards removing beetroot stains.

This stuff is so useful – I sneak it into all sorts of recipes. You can buy it in Middle Eastern stores, but it takes just 10 minutes to make your own…

Place the water in a pan, add the sugar and bring to the boil. Bubble for 10 minutes, remove from the heat and add the vinegar. When it is a bit cooler, add the mint, bottle and chill.

MOROCCAN RAW TURNIP SALAD

CRUNCHY *MEZE*
FOR 4 (OR A SUPER-
HEALTHY WINTER
LUNCH FOR
1 VIRTUOUS SOUL)

5 tbsp good olive oil

juice and grated zest of 1 lime

½ tsp ground cumin

1 tsp ground coriander

½ tsp ground cinnamon

1 tsp ground paprika

1 tsp dried dill

salt

4 pert-looking baby turnips,
    peeled and very thinly sliced

50g/1¾ oz/½ cup flaked
    (slivered) almonds

1 small pomegranate (really
    juicy, preferably Iranian or
    Turkish)

big bunch of watercress

1 medium red onion, cut
    into slices

½ tsp ground black pepper

'Do not crawl into a turnip furrow and open your mouth: the turnip cannot accompany you in wit or on journeys...' Rumi

... it is, however, really healthy fare, even when cooked. The turnip is a much overlooked little chap, but it is cheap, full of nutrients and great for chesty colds. We should be eating it more often.

Raw stuff. It's real fashionable at the mo – and by all accounts much better for us. But if I am honest, I still experience a little frisson of danger every time I eat something raw that I have spent my life eating cooked. This turnip salad recipe is a good example.

It is based on something I had in Morocco (um, hence the name of the dish), but improvised with an added Persian twist. It is pleasingly red, white and green, and so would make for good yuletide fare.

Whisk 3 tablespoons of the olive oil together with the lime juice, spices, dill and a pinch of salt. Place the turnips in a plastic bowl and cover them with the spiced oil. Mix well, cover and chill for 1–2 hours.

Put the almonds on a baking tray and toast in the oven (at 190°C/375°F/Gas mark 5) for around 10 minutes, or until lightly golden in colour.

Just before you are ready to eat, pummel the pomegranate all over with your thumbs, taking care not to break the skin: it should end up quite soft and squidgy under the skin. Make a small incision in the skin and invert the hole made over a glass: if you squeeze very gently, the juice released by your pummelling should flow into the glass. Now that the tension is released, you should be able to break the fruit open and scoop all the intact, remaining seeds into a bowl (take care not to include any pith).

Pile some watercress into your salad bowl, then scatter some of the marinated turnips (and the marinade) over it. Top with some of the onion and pomegranate seeds, and repeat until all the ingredients have been layered up. Finally, scatter the almonds over the top.

Beat the remaining olive oil together with the extracted pomegranate juice, black pepper and salt to taste, and then drizzle it over the salad.

MARINATED ASPARAGUS

MEZE OR REFINED
SNACKING FOR 4–6

1–2 bunches of asparagus,
   woody white end bits
   lopped off

100ml/3½ fl oz/scant ½ cup
   extra-virgin olive oil

juice and grated zest of 2 lemons

2 garlic cloves, minced

sea salt and freshly ground
   black pepper

2 tsp *za'atar* (see p.16), optional

Some vegetables are so extraordinarily special that they do not brook much fancy meddling. One such is asparagus.

Although the word is derived from the Persian word *asparagh* (sprout), it is not commonly enjoyed in the Middle East. But it has been popular around the Mediterranean for centuries and the Romans couldn't get enough of it.

Blanch the asparagus in boiling water for around 3 minutes before draining and plunging into icy cold water.

Whisk the oil, lemon, garlic, seasoning and *za'atar* together. Place the drained asparagus in a tub, bathe it in the marinade, cover and chill for 2–3 hours. Share, if you must.

AVOCADO AND YOGURT DIP WITH SUMAC

Ah now. Avocado. Known across the region as, um, avocado. It is certainly not indigenous to the Middle East, but it has nevertheless become ubiquitous across the region over the last 100 years or so. And it is via Israel that avocados came to the UK. Bizarrely, I can remember my mother going to a product launch party for housewives in the 1970s: it was organised by Carmel with a view to introducing this wondrous new 'fruit'. I guess it made a change from Tupperware and coffee mornings. Not that she'll admit to having attended such things.

Not only is avocado tasty, slightly posh and a very pretty shade of green, it is good for you. It is very oily, but the oil is all good stuff, and the fruit is now widely believed to reduce cholesterol. Inclusion of more avocado in your diet (reputedly) has long-term benefits for both skin and hair.

Sumac has slightly antibacterial properties, and if you use a good live yogurt to boot, that makes this a really healthy snack.

Peel the avocados and remove the stones. Plop them in a blender along with all the other ingredients and whizz for a few seconds. I like this dip all artisan and chunky, but if you want homogenised, then blend it a bit more.

Garnish with some extra sprinkled sumac and serve with hot pitta bread and crudités. Or if you are a peasant like myself, you could just eat it with a spoon straight from the bowl.

MAKES ENOUGH FOR
A BIG BOWLFUL

2 large ripe avocados
  (or 3–4 small ones)
250g/9oz/generous 1 cup thick,
  plain live yogurt
2 tomatoes (softish ones will do),
  quartered
2 garlic cloves, peeled
big handful of fresh coriander
  (cilantro)
½ tsp ground cumin
½ tsp ground coriander
1 generous tsp ground sumac,
  plus extra to garnish
½ tsp chilli powder (or more if
  you're a bit of a chilli-head)
grated zest and juice of 1 lime
glug of olive oil
salt, to taste

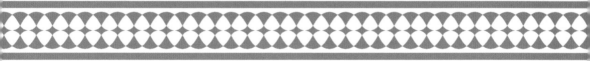

Maash Pulao

SPICED BROWN RICE AND MUNG BEAN SALAD

Maash Pulao is a popular Afghan dish, although it is also enjoyed across Transoxiana (north-eastern Iran and Central Asia). But the dish is generally served hot, with or without meaty bits added. Here it is turned into something else entirely.

Rice salad at buffet parties, frankly, used to give me the willies. Boiled Uncle Ben's with some defrosted frozen vegetables shoved up it. You should find this *meze*/lunchbox filler altogether more interesting…

SIDE DISH OR *MEZE*
PLATTER FOR 6
250g/9oz/1¼ cups brown basmati rice
75g/2¾ oz/scant ½ cup dried apricots
100g/3½ oz/½ cup mung beans
butter (or ghee) and salt
2 good tsp garam masala
1 bunch of spring onions (scallions), chopped
80g/3oz radishes, sliced

80g/3oz/½ cup halved pistachio kernels (or use pumpkin seed kernels)
2 tbsp mango pickle (yes, you can substitute another pickle – mango is just better)
3 tbsp olive oil
1 tbsp apple vinegar
salt and freshly ground black pepper
½ bunch of fresh coriander (cilantro), chopped

Soak the rice for around 30 minutes: this is not essential, but in the case of brown rice it does make for a softer end product/less cooking time. At the same time, set the apricots to soak in a separate bowl of water.

Put the mung beans in a pan of cold water and bring to the boil; they take about 25 minutes to cook.

While the beans are cooking, boil or steam the rice with butter and salt according to your preferred method.* Drain if necessary, stir the garam masala through it, mixing thoroughly, and set it aside to cool.

Meanwhile, back in the bean pan: you should cook the mung beans until they are edible without being mushy, then run some cold water over them to arrest the cooking process. Drain and reserve.

Drain and chop the apricots and mix them with the cooled rice, beans, onions, radishes and nuts in a bowl. Whisk the pickle, oil and vinegar together with a little salt and pepper and pour it over the *Maash Pulao*, stirring well. Finally, toss the coriander through the salad: this is done at the last moment to preserve the pretty green-ness of the herbs. Check the seasoning and serve. This is one of my favourite shopkeeper lunches: full of good things, easily digestible and no garlic to scare the customers away.

* Handy tip
Here's my preferred general-purpose method for cooking rice, if it helps: Use 1 measure of rice to 1 measure of water (a standard rice cup holds around 150g/5½oz/¾ cup of rice and 200ml/7fl oz/¾ cup of water) plus 2 teaspoons butter (or ghee) and salt to taste. Rinse the rice well. Put the water, butter and salt in a pan and bring it to the boil. Add the rice, bubble away for a few minutes, then turn down the heat really low, wrap the lid of the pan in a clean cloth and simmer for another 20 minutes. The rice should be perfectly cooked and the grains perfectly separated. Let it sit, covered, for 5–10 minutes more before fluffing with a fork and serving.

GIANT COUSCOUS AND BLACK CUMIN SALAD

SERVES 6

olive oil, for frying

1 good tsp black cumin seeds

½ tsp chilli (red pepper) flakes

about 1.5cm/⅝in piece fresh
ginger, peeled and minced

200g/7oz giant couscous

around 500ml/18fl oz/generous
2 cups good vegetable stock
(or good water)

3 tbsp extra-virgin olive oil

2 tsp *pekmez* (grape syrup)

1 tbsp balsamic vinegar

salt

1 bunch of spring onions
(scallions), chopped

½ bunch of fresh coriander (cilantro), chopped

around 24 dates, pitted and
roughly chopped

120g/4oz *labneh* balls,
roughly crumbled

The black cumin myth

This is regular cumin's frightfully elite cousin. It is also known as black caraway. Black cumin is not the same as *Nigella sativa*, and neither of these are related to the *Allium* family, which makes the nickname 'black onion seeds' (with which both get labelled) confusing at best. Black cumin is slightly sweet, packed full of nutrients and aids the digestion. It is used mostly in Iranian and Central Asian cuisine, and is deployed to great effect in *zireh pulao*, a fragrant rice dish.

Well, this has got our shop and supper club customers talking, and so we thought we'd share the recipe with you. It is spicy, filling and healthy, and so it's perfect for winter snacking. It also makes a great *meze* dish.

Giant couscous is also known as Israeli couscous, but is confusingly not as giant as *moghrabbieh*, its Levantine cousin. It is easier to work with than moghrabbieh, as it is not as starchy, but it gets just as many 'oohs' and 'aahs' when you dish it up as it looks, well, like toy food. Not entirely real.

You can of course make this recipe with any number of grains in place of the couscous. And if you can't get *labneh*, just use feta in its place. Black cumin seeds have a fairly unique flavour, but if you can't find them, substitute green cumin and caraway seeds. Oh and finally, if you can't find *pekmez* (which is available at all good Greek and Turkish shops), replace it with pomegranate paste, or (if you're desperate) brown sauce mixed with extra balsamic vinegar. Why so many alternative ingredient ideas? Because food should never be that stressy, and you should never be slave to a recipe: if you can't get the right stuff, cheat.

So all you do is... heat the oil in a saucepan and toss in the spices and ginger, stirring constantly. Have the extractor fan on or the window open, as sizzling chilli can make you choke. After 30 seconds, add the couscous, mixing well. Turn it over in the oil until it starts to brown, then trickle in a little of the stock (just as you would with a risotto). Once the liquid has been absorbed, add a little bit more; repeat until the couscous has swollen and softened. This process should take no more than 20 minutes. Wrap the lid of the pan in a clean cloth, turn the heat off and let the contents 'sweat' for a further 10 minutes before setting the pan aside somewhere to cool.

Once it has cooled to room temperature or thereabouts, whisk the extra-virgin olive oil, *pekmez*, balsamic vinegar and salt together and pour it over the couscous, stirring well, then add the rest of the ingredients. (By dressing it first then adding the herbs and cheese, the contrasting colours will be preserved for a little longer.)

Serve with warm bread for supper, or as part of a *meze*. Or spoon it into your finest Tupperware for lunch tomorrow.

WARM AUBERGINE SALAD
WITH CHILLIED *TAHINI*

Aubergines and *tahini*: a match made in *jannah* (Arabic heaven). Aubergine is to all intents and purposes edible blotting paper: it absorbs any flavours you care to chuck at it.

SNACK SUPPER FOR 2:
ALSO GOOD FOR LADIES
WHO *MEZE*-LUNCH
2 medium aubergines (eggplants),
    cut into 2–3cm/¾–1¼ in cubes
2 small red onions,
    cut into 2–3cm/¾–1¼ in cubes
olive oil
1–1½ tsp lemon salt (citric acid)
6 garlic cloves (less if you have an important
    meeting in the morning), peeled and
    'bruised' (bash swiftly with the flat part
    of a chopping knife)

3 tbsp *tahina*
1 tbsp lemon juice
around 150ml/5fl oz/⅔ cup cold water
½ tsp chilli (red pepper) flakes
salt, to taste
1–2 tbsp sesame seeds (2 if you are like me
    and can never get enough of the things)
big handful of fresh parsley and mint, chopped

Preheat the oven to 180°C/350°F/Gas mark 4.

Arrange the aubergines and onions on a baking tray. Drizzle with olive oil, sprinkle with the lemon salt and bake uncovered for around 20 minutes; then add the garlic and cook for a further 20 minutes, or until the vegetables are tender and turning brown.

Meanwhile, whisk the *tahina* together with the lemon juice and beat in enough cold water to make a drizzle-able paste. Add the chilli flakes and salt as required, and chill until needed. Time too to toast the sesame seeds: dry-fry them for a few minutes until they start to brown then set aside.

When the aubergine is cooked, arrange it on a plate. Trickle the *tahini* over it, then sprinkle with sesame seeds and chopped herbs. Serve with warm moppy bread.

Salata Duco

SAUDI CORIANDER SALSA

This is sooo simple. Easy-peasy lemon-and-lime-squeezy. It is pretty moreish eaten on its own, but it makes a great cooling accompaniment to other rich meze plates, not to mention kebabs. It is the Arabian answer to *fattoush*, the classic Lebanese dish made with stale bread, or *salad-e-Shirazi*, which is the quintessential Persian salad, made like *ducos*, but with onion and cucumber as well.

Sear the tomatoes over a lit gas ring, or plunge them into boiling water: either method will have the desired result of allowing you to peel them (probably best let them cool a little first). Chop the tomato flesh finely into a bowl, taking care to retain all the juice.

Roughly chop the coriander, chillies and garlic if using, then pound them together with the salt in a pestle and mortar. If you don't own a pestle and mortar (I don't, but don't tell any of my foodie friends), then put the herb/chilli/garlic/salt mixture on a chopping board, cover it with a clean cloth and grind it using a chunky utensil handle. Mix the resultant green gloop into the tomatoes and dress with the lime or lemon juice. Add more salt as required. Best consumed within a few hours.

MAKES A WEE BOWLFUL

4 large tomatoes (soft ones will do nicely)
small bunch of fresh coriander (cilantro), trimmed
2–3 green chillies
2 garlic cloves, peeled (optional)
½ tsp salt (celery salt works best here, but is not authentic)
juice of 2 limes (or lemons)

CABBAGE WITH SUMAC

To make a healthy change from coleslaw: in addition to its obvious casting as part of a *meze* spread, this performs well at barbecues. This is based on a Georgian recipe.

Blanch the cabbage in boiling water for just 1 minute before draining then plunging it into cold water to arrest the cooking process. Drain it once again and put it in a bowl.

Next, whisk the olive oil together with the garlic, sumac and seasoning and pour it over the cabbage, stirring well. Cover the bowl and leave it in the fridge for 2 hours.

Just before you're ready to serve, dry toast the hemp (or sesame) and caraway seeds in a small pan for a minute or so. Arrange the cabbage (marinade 'n' all) on a pretty plate and sprinkle with the still-warm seeds.

MEZE FOR 4

around 600g/1lb 5oz (roughly half a head) cabbage, shredded (red, green or white ... or all three if you're feeling extravagant)
50ml/1¾ fl oz/scant ¼ cup extra-virgin olive oil
2 garlic cloves, minced
1½ tsp sumac
sea salt and freshly ground black pepper (according to preference)
1 tbsp hemp seeds (or use sesame)
1 level tsp caraway seeds

Mostly Carbs

Mana'eesh

LEBANESE STREET PIZZA BREAD

MAKES 15

For the basic dough:

7g/¼ oz sachet dried yeast (or use about 12g/scant ½ oz fresh)

pinch of sugar

250ml/9fl oz/generous 1 cup lukewarm water

500g/1lb 2oz/3½ cups plain (all-purpose) flour

1 tsp salt

1–2 tbsp olive oil

Mana'eesh is a popular Lebanese street snack: part open sandwich, part mini pizza. At its simplest, it is just a particularly flavoursome bread. Get creative and you've got a whole range of canapés, picnic and party possibilities open to you.

I offer three toppings: the first is the most traditional, *za'atar*. The second is a Syrian version, using the *dukkah* topping. The third, *laham b'ajeen*, involves minced lamb (p.129).

Dissolve the yeast and sugar in the warm water and set aside for 10 minutes.

Sift the flour and salt into a mixing bowl and make a well in the middle. Now add the yeast-water combo, mixing at first with a wooden spoon, then, when the ingredients come together, your hands. Form the dough into a ball and roll it in a little oil to keep it moist. Cover it with a damp cloth and leave somewhere warm for 2 hours to rise.

When risen, knead the mixture with verve, vim and vigour on a floured work surface, then divide it into 15 balls. Leave the dough to rise for a further 15 minutes, then pull them into small flat rounds with your hands and spread them out on 1 or 2 oiled baking trays.

Preheat the oven to 230°C/450°F/Gas mark 8.

Bake the bread rounds for 8–10 minutes, or until they are slightly risen and lightly browned. These will keep for several days in a covered plastic tub, and can be eaten hot or cold. This bread/pastry is kinda soft, and so can also be warmed in a microwave.

ZA'ATAR TOPPING

Za'atar is one of the most famous Middle Eastern spice/condiment blends. Every town and village across the Levant makes it differently, but it is basically a mixture of wild thyme (which is in itself known as *za'atar*) with sumac, sesame and salt. You can buy it easily enough in good Middle Eastern stores now, but it is also simple to make. Grind 2 parts thyme (in the absence of real wild thyme) with 1 part sumac, a handful of sesame seeds and salt to taste. To turn it into a distinctive and aromatic bread or pizza topping, mix the spices with olive oil to form a paste, then smear the paste across the raw *mana'eesh* dough just before you cook it. The addition of grated mozzarella or halloumi is an authentic optional extra.

DUKKAH: A REALLY TOP TOPPING

Dukkah is used both as a condiment in Arabic countries and as a snack in its own right. It is basically a coarse-ground spicy nut/seed mix, but it is very tasty and can be used in all sorts of culinary contexts. The original recipe calls for equal quantities of raw hazelnuts and sesame seeds, together with half that amount of cumin and coriander seeds. You toast all the ingredients together, then crush them coarsely and season to taste with sea salt and coarsely ground black pepper. For this recipe, I vary it slightly by using 50g/1¾oz/⅓ cup each of sunflower, sesame and pumpkin seeds, and 50g/1¾oz/⅓ cup hazelnuts or almonds. Add 1 tbsp each of cumin, coriander and fenugreek seeds, then toast, season and blend.

Injera
ETHIOPIAN PANCAKE BREAD

Injera is a lot more than a bread: it is a whole concept and one that is seminal to the Ethiopian way of eating. Ethiopian cooking is one of the most exciting cuisines in the world, as it has remained largely uncorrupted by the scourge of colonisation.

Injera is a really friendly, fun-loving carbohydrate. You see, it's used as a tablecloth: an edible tablecloth. You just plonk it on top of a little (traditionally round, low-lying) table, and ladle your food on top. No knives or forks or plates: no washing-up. Just break off a bit of the tablecloth, and use it to scoop up the dish of your choice. Perfect for *meze* and snacking. In Ethiopia, it is usually served with wat, or stew, but we like to dot it with dips, salads and marinated vegetables.

It is traditionally made from *teff*, a teensy-weensy millet-like grain. *Teff* has been grown in East Africa for thousands of years, and is particularly suited to the nomadic lifestyle as it springs up pretty quickly and doesn't need pampered soil in which to do its thing. It's nigh on impossible to find in the West, but the flavour and the experience is easily replicated using flour and fizzy water.

This version is pleasingly easy to make: no faffing around with yeast, which I always find a little nerve-wracking, no need to leave the dough to ferment, and no need even for an oven.

MAKES ENOUGH FOR
A SNACK DINNER FOR 4
100g/3½ oz/¾ cup self-raising flour
100g/3½ oz/scant ⅔ cup wholewheat flour
1 tsp baking powder

pinch of salt
400ml/14fl oz/1¾ cups sparkling water/soda
juice of 1 lemon
a smidge of vegetable oil

Sift the first four ingredients together, then mix in the fizzy water and the lemon juice, beating to a smooth paste. If it is too thick, just add a little more water.

Using a brush or a piece of kitchen paper, coat a large non-stick frying pan with oil and put it on the heat. Drizzle the batter mix in, swirling it from the centre out to the edge until the bottom of the pan is evenly covered. Allow it to cook through until little holes start to appear on the surface, then remove from the pan with a wooden spatula. The result should be just cooked through on the bottom, but still spongy on top. Keep the cooked *injera* warm by covering with foil until you are ready to serve.

Repeat with the rest of the mixture – you should have enough for about 5–6 breads, which you can then piecemeal together to make a quilted spread.

Injera will keep until the next day if you wrap it in a clean cloth or plastic bag.

Mujadarra
RICE AND LENTILS

This I could probably live on. It is the sort of food that you just have to keep on eating until you are fit to pop.

Mujadarra is actually the Arabic word for smallpox. But you should not let this put you off – it merely refers to the appearance of the rice studded with lentils. It has in all likelihood been eaten for millennia in the Middle East, although the original dish was almost certainly made with bulghur wheat rather than rice. An ancient urban myth has it that this is the original 'mess of pottage' for which Esau sold his soul in the Bible. There are many versions: in Iran, *adass pulao* (spiced rice with lentils and fried fruit) is served as an accompaniment, while in Egypt *kushari* (rice, lentils and pasta) is one of the nation's favourite street foods.

It is simple and cheap to make: perfect thrifty student, comfort or snack fare.

COMFORT EATING FOR 4–6
250g/9oz/1¼ cups brown lentils
4 medium onions, peeled
oil, for frying
1 tsp ground coriander

1 tsp ground cumin
250g/9oz/1¼ cups long-grain brown rice
salt and freshly ground black pepper
generous knob of butter (or vegan alternative)

Put the lentils in a pan of unsalted water, bring it to the boil, then turn down the heat and simmer for about 15 minutes before draining and setting aside.

Finely chop 2 of the onions and fry them in a little oil. Once they have turned translucent, add the spices and rice, stirring well, followed by the par-cooked lentils. Add just enough water to the pan to only just cover the contents, then bring to the boil, turn down the heat and simmer for around 20 minutes, or until all the water has been absorbed (use a heat diffuser here if you have one – it helps when you are cooking stuff, such as rice and wheat, slowly and by absorption). Now turn off the heat and season the rice mix to taste. Wrap the lid of the pan in a clean tea towel and cover the *mujadarra*: it will continue to cook in its own steam while you set the table, feed the cat, light a candle, whatever…

To serve, slice the remaining 2 onions and fry them in butter until they are quite well browned. Pile the lentilly rice into a dish, top with the buttery onions and serve with pickles, yogurt and salad.

Laham b'ajeen
PIQUANT LAMB TOPPED PIZZAS

I am very fond of these little pizza pies. One or two make a great snack, and every shop on London's Edgware Road seems to sell them.

Fry the onion in a splosh of oil. Once it has softened, add the tomatoes and cook through so that most of the tomato juice evaporates. Add the spices and pomegranate molasses (or lemon juice), take off the heat and cool to room temperature.

Preheat the oven to 230°C/450°F/Gas mark 8.

Mix the raw minced lamb with the cooled onion mix, seasoning and pine nuts, pounding well. Form the dough into 15 small circles, as per the recipe on p.124, and distribute the raw lamb mix between them, spreading it thinly. Bake for around 10 minutes, or until sizzling and brown around the edges. Eat hot or cold: if you are enjoying them fresh out of the oven, try rolling them around a handful of fresh herbs (see p.142). They will keep for 1–2 days in the fridge.

MAKES AROUND 15

1 large onion, chopped
oil, for cooking
3 large tomatoes, chopped
1 tsp ground allspice
½ tsp ground chilli (optional)
2 tbsp pomegranate molasses
   (or lemon juice)
350g/12oz minced (ground)
   lamb (leaner cuts are better
   for this)
½ tsp salt
½ tsp ground black pepper
60g/2¼ oz/scant ½ cup pine nuts
1 quantity *mana'eesh* dough,
   pounded and proved (p.124)

SEEDED BROCCOLI SFIHA

MAKES 15

50g/1¾ oz/scant ⅓ cup raisins

2 medium heads of broccoli, broken into small florets

2 medium red onions, finely sliced

oil, for frying

2 garlic cloves, minced (optional)

2 tbsp balsamic vinegar

1 tsp brown sugar

salt and freshly ground black pepper

1 quantity *mana'eesh* dough, pounded and proved (p.124)

grated halloumi or mozzarella (optional non-vegan topping)

2–3 tbsp *dukkah* mix (see p.124)

Sfiha is yet another version of *mana'eesh*, this time from Syria. It uses the same dough, but is formed more like an eccentric tart. The conventional filling is lamb, as per the *Laham b'ajeen* recipe on p.129, but I like this veggie/vegan version.

Soak the raisins while you make the rest of the filling.

Blanch the broccoli in boiling water for around 2 minutes, then drain and refresh it under cold water.

Fry the onions in a little oil until they are soft and nicely browned, then add the garlic and (drained) raisins, stirring well for 2 minutes. Next, add the vinegar and sugar and a little seasoning, and let the mixture bubble gently for about 5 minutes before taking off the heat.

Preheat the oven to 230°C/450°F/Gas mark 8. Lightly oil a couple of baking trays.

Divide your proved *mana'eesh* dough into about 15 balls and allow them to rise for another 10 minutes before pulling and pressing them into flat discs. Put a spoonful of broccoli in the middle of each, followed by a covering of the caramelised onion mixture. Sprinkle a little grated cheese on top, if using. Taking one of the discs, pinch the edges of the dough in four places so that it folds up to form a square-ish tart (the rim should be just 5–6mm/¼in high), and slide it on to the baking tray. Repeat with the rest of the *sfiha* and bake them for around 15 minutes, or until the pastry is just starting to turn a pleasant golden colour. Remove from the oven, sprinkle liberally with *dukkah*, and serve hot, warm or cold. These keep for 2–3 days in the fridge.

GARLIC, AUBERGINE AND GINGER *PAKORA*

SERVES 8

2 large aubergines (eggplants)

salt

250g/9oz/1¾ cups chickpea
(gram) flour

½ tsp ground ginger

½ tsp ground cumin

1 tsp ground coriander

1 tsp mustard seeds

½ tsp ground fenugreek (nice,
but optional)

½ tsp ground black pepper

pinch of salt

about ⅔ can ginger beer

4 garlic cloves

sunflower or rapeseed (canola)
oil, for frying

Pakora are fritters. Spicy fritters. Yup – just like the ones you get up the Indian after a night in the pub. Except these ones are based on an Afghan recipe. They are popular street food in the main -istans, and are very easy to make at home. You can of course make them with any vegetable.

Cut the aubergines into slices of 1cm/½in thickness, arrange them on a tray and rub them with a scant amount of salt. Set them aside for around 30 minutes.

Make the batter: sift the flour into a bowl with the spices and seasoning and slowly add the ginger beer, whisking all the while. This too will benefit from 30 minutes' 'rest'.

Ready to cook? Wipe the aubergine firmly with some kitchen paper, then chop the garlic with ½ teaspoon salt and rub the mixture over the aubergine slices. Whisk up the batter again, and heat at least 4cm/1½in oil in a frying pan. Dip the aubergine into the batter, allowing any surplus to drain back into the bowl, and fry each of the slices off until they are golden brown. Drain on kitchen paper and serve hot with chutney or yogurt. These are best eaten fresh as they don't reheat very well.

Manti

KAZAKH DUMPLINGS

Mmmm. Dumplings. This is another recipe with decidedly oriental overtones: it is most likely that the dish was first created by the Uighurs in Western China, and travelled (perhaps with that enterprising chappy Ghengis Khan, who spread culture and terror in equal measure) west to Central Asia. The Turkic nations also seem mighty fond of it, which is why it crops up in Turkey and Armenia. The original ingredients almost certainly comprised horsemeat, which remains popular in the region, but as we live in a nation of hippophiles and in the interests of keeping my shop windows intact, I have substituted lamb.

MAKES ABOUT 24

FOR THE PASTA:
400g/14oz/scant 3 cups plain
    (all-purpose) flour
1 level tsp salt
175ml/6fl oz/¾ cup cold water

FOR THE FILLING:
400g/14oz coarsely minced (ground) lamb
1 onion, grated
2 green chillies, finely chopped
1 bunch of fresh coriander (cilantro), chopped
1 level tsp ground cumin
salt and freshly ground black pepper
50g/1¾oz/3½ tbsp butter, cut into 24 cubes

Sift the flour and salt into a mixing bowl and trickle in the water, mixing with a wooden spoon, to form a stiff dough. Knead it with your hands for 5–10 minutes, then roll it into a ball, cover with a damp cloth and let it rest for an hour. You may do the same if you wish.

To make the filling, squidge the lamb together with all the other ingredients apart from the butter, pounding well so that the heat from your hands 'warms' the fat of the lamb (this will help the flavours to mingle better).

When you are ready to cook the *manti*, scatter some flour on your work surface, divide the dough into 2 balls, roll each one out into an oblong about 2mm/1⁄16 in thick, then use a circular pastry cutter (8cm/3¼in diameter is ideal, or you can improvise with a jar lid). Put a dollop of the mince mixture on one side of each one, dot it with a lump of butter and fold the other semi-circle over to form a pocket. Crimp the edges loosely with your fingers to seal the *manti*.

Quarter fill a steamer with water and bring it to the boil on the hob. If you do not have a patent steaming device, all is not lost: you can improvise with a lidded colander (or stack of them) set over a pan of boiling water. Grease the parts of the basket (or colander) which will come into contact with the dough, and carefully arrange the dumplings inside. If your steamer has only one layer, then you will need to cook the *manti* in 2–3 batches. Steam them for about 40 minutes, and serve hot or cold with yogurt* or chilli sauce.

*BONUS RECIPE: QUICK YOGURT SAUCE
Mix about 200g/7oz plain yogurt with 5–6 minced garlic cloves, 75ml/5 tbsp cold water plus salt and freshly ground black pepper to taste. Add 1 tbsp chopped dill (optional). Couldn't really be any simpler.

Çörek
TURKISH MILK BREAD WITH SESAME

Most countries have a version of this: a soft, glazed, egg-enriched bread, a bit like brioche, or *cholla*, or what in Iran is known as *naan sheermal*. Now I am a self-confessed butter glutton, but this stuff is really rather cakey, and pretty addictive all on its own. It is also a great dunker: try it with coffee, or chocolate, or just with warm spiced milk...

In Turkey, *çörek* is most often to be found starring in a breakfast role: it can be made as a savoury roll, or, as here, a sweet, seeded plait.

SATES 4–6

1 sachet (7g/¼ oz) dried yeast
   (or 15g/½ oz fresh)
150ml/5fl oz/²/₃ cup warm milk
100g/3½ oz/½ cup sugar
450g/1lb/scant 3¼ cups plain
   (all-purpose) flour
½ tsp salt
1 level tsp ground cinnamon

2 eggs, beaten
150g/5½ oz/scant ¾ cup butter, softened

FOR THE GLAZE/TOPPING:
¼ tsp ground saffron dissolved in
   1 tbsp boiling water
1 egg, beaten
2 tbsp hulled sesame seeds
2 tsp nigella seeds

Dissolve the yeast in the warm milk together with 50g/1¾oz of the sugar, and set it aside for 10 minutes to do its thing.

Sift the rest of the sugar into a bowl together with the flour, salt and cinnamon and make a well in the middle. Whisk the eggs and butter, together then pour them into the well along with the yeast mix. Stir it all together with a wooden spoon, then knead with your hands until it comes together (if it looks dry, add a little cold water). Cover the bowl and leave the dough somewhere warm to rise for around 2 hours.

After 2 hours, knead the dough on a lightly floured surface for around 5 minutes more then split it into 6 or 8 lumps as required. Stretch two of these into strips of 15–20cm/ 6–8in and pinch them together at one end before plaiting them loosely. Repeat with the other pairs of strips, then leave the dough to rise again for another 15 minutes.

Sprinkle the saffron on to the boiling water and set it aside to cool. Meanwhile, preheat the oven to 190°C/375°F/Gas mark 5.

When the saffron water has cooled a little, whisk it into the egg and use a pastry brush or a wad of kitchen paper to spread the glaze over the *çörek*. Sprinkle the seeds over the plaits, then put them on to a greased baking tray and bake for around 25 minutes, or until they are a dark golden-brown colour. Enjoy warm or cold: if you store them wrapped in plastic or in an airtight plastic tub, they will keep for 4–5 days.

Sabich

ISRAELI VEGGIE DAGWOOD SANDWICH

This is my kind of sandwich: maximalist. It contains a whole pantry of potential *meze* items in one pitta pocket, creating one unfeasibly fat bite.

The ingredients for the filling of *sabich* were actually staple Sabbath fare for Iraqi Jews, many of whom entered Israel in the 1940s and 1950s. Israeli street vendors had soon turned the combo into a sandwich, and it now gives the falafel pocket a run for its shekels as the nation's favourite street food. I think of it as an aubergine sarnie, but it also contains potato, egg, pickled cucumbers, mango pickle, tomato and cucumber salad, fresh herbs, *houmous* and *tahini*. The somewhat anomalous mango pickle (*ambeh*) insinuated its way into *sabich* after voyaging from India to Iraq c/o silk route traders.

If I am making it for a few people at home, I like to serve *sabich* as a *meze* spread, popping all the ingredients in little bowls and letting folk create their own: there is something very appealing about self-assembly food.

SERVES 4

salt

1 large aubergine (eggplant), thinly sliced

2 medium waxy potatoes, scrubbed and sliced into 2mm/ 1⁄16 in rounds

oil, for frying

2 garlic cloves, sliced

2 medium tomatoes, diced

1⁄2 cucumber, finely diced

1 small onion, finely diced

1⁄2 bunch of fresh parsley, chopped

1⁄2 bunch of fresh coriander (cilantro), chopped

juice and grated zest of 1 lemon

ground black pepper

4 slices pitta bread (wholemeal is better for you, and tastier. Just saying...)

2 tbsp *houmous* (see p.106)

2 tbsp *tahini**

4 perfectly hard-boiled eggs, sliced

2 tbsp salty mango pickle

8 sliced pickled cucumbers (see p.12)

* Note on tahini

Ah, *tahini*. Well *tahina* as you buy it is famous for its cement-like texture. In order to render it into *tahini* 'sauce', you need to blend it with lemon juice, water, salt and freshly ground black pepper until it becomes pale and creamy and much more workable. It thickens in the fridge, so it is a good idea to make it a little runnier than you require. Add garlic, coriander and parsley as well, and you have a lovely moreish dip, which the Cypriots call *tashi*.

Sprinkle some salt on the aubergine slices and set aside: the salt draws the moisture and innate bitterness from the vegetable. After around 20 minutes, dab them with kitchen paper.

Fry the potatoes in a splash of oil until they are soft and golden-ish (or you can boil them until they are just cooked: this would be healthier and more authentic). Drain them on kitchen paper, then fry the garlic and aubergines in the same oil, adding more if necessary, again removing them with a slotted spoon to drain.

Mix the tomato, cucumber, onion, herbs, lemon juice, zest, pepper and some salt together.

Preheat the grill, if using. Grill or toast the pitta until it puffs up, then split it along one side to create a fillable pocket. Spread one side of the cavity of each with *houmous* and the other with *tahini*. Next, add a couple of slices of the fried aubergine and potato to each, then top these with sliced egg. Spoon some mango pickle over the egg, followed with the pickled cucumbers. Top with the salady salsa. I recommend that you eat it immediately.

Hawawshi

EGYPTIAN MINCED MEAT SARNIE

SERVES 2

300g/10½ oz minced (ground)
    beef (fatty mince works best)
1 small–medium onion, grated
1–2 garlic cloves, minced
1 large tomato, diced
1 green chilli, diced
1 level tsp ground cumin
1 level tsp dried mint
handful of fresh parsley,
    chopped
½ tsp salt
1 large *khobez* (or 2 pitta breads),
    wholemeal if possible as it is
    tastier and better for you
olive oil
1–2 tsp *dukkah* (optional
    topping)

TO SERVE:

liquid *labneh* (lightly salted thick
    yogurt will also do) or *tahini*
    (see p.136)

Now this is fun, albeit counter-kitchen-intuitive. An Egyptian *enchilada*, made with raw mince, which is then baked inside the bread. It is of course amazingly tasty, as all the dripping goodness from the meat gets soaked up by the bread. My Egyptian customers tell me that this street snack is especially popular in Alexandria. And who am I to argue?

Everyday bread in Egypt is known as *aish*, and comes in two main varieties: *aish shamsi* (made with white flour) and *aish baladi* (made with wholemeal). It is to all intents and purposes the same as the *khobez* or pitta which is now so easily available in the West, and so that is what we will use.

Preheat the oven to 190°C/375°F/Gas mark 5.

Mix the mince with the diced vegetables, chilli, cumin, herbs and salt. Pound it for a good few minutes: the warmth of your hands will soften the fat content of the meat and help the flavours mingle.

Cut the bread in half to form two semi-circles, then split each half open to form two pockets. Smear the meat mixture across the bottom layer of each pocket and press the pockets a little so that they 'close'. Brush the outside of the bread with a dobbin of oil, and sprinkle some *dukkah* on top if you have some handy.

Now wrap the *hawawshi* in baking parchment and pop them on a baking tray. Bake for about 15 minutes, then turn the sandwiches over and bake for a further 15 minutes, or until the bread is crispy and the meat sizzling.

Serve with a drizzle of *labneh* or *tahini* sauce. They are astonishingly moreish.

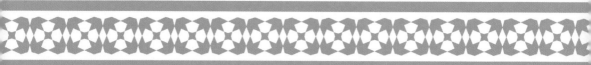

PERSIAN-STYLE HERB WRAP

SERVES 1

a handful of flatbread (*lavash* or
  village bread: the sort that
  you don't need to heat)
labneh or cream cheese
  (my addition: I am not a
  hardcore herbivore like
  Mr. Shopkeeper)
a handful of herbs or salad leaves

This simple Persian fare is my simple* Persian husband's third favourite snackette. See, we always keep a big basket of herbs at home (of which more in the note on p.142). So if he's in a big hurry, or my wifely failings have left a slight hiatus in the snack provisions department, he will gorge on this. It is surprisingly satisfying, and obviously much healthier than his first favourite snackette (which consists of most of Chapter Three). Its other great virtue is that it takes about three seconds to assemble.

  *Simple in tastes, only. Let it be known that in every other respect he is far cleverer than I.

Rip off a strip of bread. Smear it with *labneh*. Grab a handful of herbs and wrap the bread around it. End of.

FALAFEL POCKET: THE DEFINITIVE MIDDLE-EASTERN SANDWICH

Falafel. They were probably created in Egypt, made Israel their spiritual home, and have now conquered the world. And they are about the only late-night veggie option for post-pub munchies (although there is always chips and cheese). When they are fresh, moist and perfectly cooked, they are a delight. If they are dry or overcooked, frankly I wouldn't even give them to Master Shopcat.

To make the perfect falafel sarnie, apart from perfect falafel you also need the perfect extras: piquant sauce, fresh salad, pert pickles and crisp but not too crisp bread. If you are at home, it is rather fun to re-create that greasy vegan spoon experience by putting a range of possible fillings out and inviting people to build their own sandwiches. In fact, you could even cook the falafel at the table, like a fondue – although that might be a bit messy/dangerous.

PER PERSON:
1 pitta bread (wholemeal is tastier, really)
3 hot fresh falafel (shop bought or see below)

OPTIONAL EXTRAS:
Kebab Salad Mix (p.55)
tahini (see p.136 – you'll need about 2 tbsp per person)
extra special chilli sauce (see right – again, about 2 tbsp per person)

Avocado and Yogurt Dip with Sumac (p.115)
houmous (see p.106)
grilled halloumi
fried baby cauliflower florets
fried aubergine (eggplant) slices
fried potatoes (AKA chips/fries)
fried beetroot chips
pickled cucumbers or mixed pickle (see p.10 or 12)
lemon wedges

The only secret with this falafel banquet is to serve all the hot stuff hot. So get it all ready, and keep it warm until needed.

FALAFEL REFRESHER COURSE
What? You want to know how to make falafel as well? Oh – alright then. To make about 15: soak 150g/5½oz/scant 1 cup each of dried chickpeas and dried split broad beans (or just use chickpeas) in water overnight. Drain and blend with ½ teaspoon each bicarbonate of soda (baking soda) and chilli powder, and 1 teaspoon ground cumin, ½ bunch each of chopped parsley and coriander (cilantro), 1 large onion, 4–5 garlic cloves and salt to taste. If the mixture's too wet, add flour; if too dry, add water. Form into balls and deep-fry until they are golden brown and float on the surface. Drain on kitchen paper. Sorted.

BONUS RECIPE: EXTRA-SPECIAL CHILLI SAUCE
If you're a bit of a kebab head, or enjoy this sort of snack on a regular basis, keeping a bottle of this homemade chilli sauce in the fridge is a fine idea. Fry 2 medium chopped onions with 5–6 chopped garlic cloves, 2 chopped Scotch bonnet chillies (or 6–7 green chillies), 1 diced green (bell) pepper and 2 chopped sticks of celery. When soft, add 1 tsp ground coriander, ½ tsp cinnamon, ½ tsp cumin and 1 heaped tsp tomato paste. Stir well for a few minutes, then add 2 cans (400g/14oz) tomato concasse (chopped tomatoes), and 4 tbsp pomegranate molasses. Simmer for about 10 minutes, season to taste, blend, cool and bottle in sterilised jars (see p.10) until needed.

Sarnweech-e-Zaban

IRANIAN TONGUE SANDWICH

SERVES 2

2 small baguettes

6 Iranian-style pickled
     cucumbers (see p.12),
     finely sliced lengthways

2 nice tomatoes, finely sliced

big handful of fresh parsley and
     coriander (cilantro), chopped

small handful of shredded lettuce

2 cooked lambs' tongues, sliced

salt and freshly ground
     black pepper

2 lemon wedges

Offal is big in the Middle East. Nothing gets wasted – sheep feet, brains and heads, sheep or calves liver, heart and kidneys… and tongue. We do of course have a long history of eating tongue in the West, but it is not perhaps as widespread as it once was (yup – we are getting squeamish), and certainly not in the sphere of fast food.

  Iranian sandwiches (which are rather sweetly known as *sarnweech*) are made with small French-style baguettes, and come in eight or nine popular varieties, all with the same accompaniments: they do not use sauce, or butter, or mayonnaise, so what you get is just meat and/or vegetable goodness. Tongue is the most popular; the *sarnweech-e-zaban* is practically a street-food institution.

Split the baguettes lengthways, line with the pickles, cucumber, tomato, herbs and lettuce. Sprinkle the tongue with salt and pepper and arrange it on top of the salad filling. Add lemon as required. And that's it.

A note on herbs

Most Iranian households keep a big basket of washed and sorted *sabzi khordan* (literally: herbs for eating) in their fridge: these make an appearance at lunch and dinner, as great handfuls of herbs are eaten as an appetiser and an aid to digestion. The selection usually comprises fresh parsley, mint, coriander (cilantro), basil, cress, chives and tarragon, along with spring onions (scallions) and radishes. It is also very handy to keep such a resource for cooking purposes: we could all do with eating (and growing) more herbs. Washed herbs keep well in a colander or plastic bag in the fridge for around 5 days.

HOW TO COOK A TONGUE

Lambs' tongues are readily available from good independent butchers. When you get them home, clean them as best you can, and put them in a pan with water, chopped celery, onion, bay leaves, black peppercorns and a handful of chickpeas (which serve to absorb any 'strong' cooking smells). Bring to the boil, turn down the heat and simmer for 2–3 hours (more if you want to enjoy them as a casserole), keeping an eye on the liquid levels: add salt right at the end (adding it too soon makes the meat tough). Remove the tongue from the cooking stock and allow to cool a little before peeling off the outer skin. Chill well before slicing. If you have children at home, it is fun to leave the tongues really visible in the fridge: you will then be met with a barrage of 'Eurgh! Gross!' as you snigger in the next room.

Halwah: Sweet Treats

Umm Ali
ALI'S MOTHER'S PUDDING

SERVES 6

around 350g/12oz (raw weight)
frozen or chilled puff pastry
(filo/phyllo will do) or 4 large
plain croissants (stale will do)
450ml/16fl oz/2 cups (or 1 can)
condensed milk
500ml/18fl oz/generous 2 cups
water
5–6 drops vanilla essence
(extract)
100g/3½ oz/¾ cup desiccated
(dry unsweetened) coconut
200g/7oz/1⅓ cups mixed nuts:
choose from flaked (slivered)
almonds, chopped pistachio
kernels, blanched, chopped
hazelnuts, pine nuts, chopped
raw cashews
125ml/4fl oz/½ cup whipping
cream, duly whipped
50g/1¾ oz/½ cup toasted flaked
almonds or nibbed
pistachios, to decorate

This is one of Egypt's favourite childhood puddings. I just love food with a story attached. Such dishes become deeply ensconced in a nation's culinary heart. This Egyptian classic comes with one of the best ancient urban legends attached...

Many centuries ago (in around 1250 AD in fact, at the time of the Crusades), Egypt was left king-less when its Sultan of the time, al-Salih Ayyoub, contracted a fever suddenly and died. His resourceful wife, a former slave by the name of Shajjar al-Durr, took over and by all accounts was pretty good in her assumed role until the Caliph of Baghdad found out. He wasn't having a woman ruler on his watch, and so he sent a chap called Aybak to marry her and help around the house/kingdom.

Shajjar al-Durr rather liked her new husband, and prevailed upon him to divorce his first wife, who went by the name of Umm Ali (Ali's mother).

Things were fine for seven years, and then Shajjar al-Durr discovered that Aybak wasn't quite the catch she'd thought he was. And so she had him killed in the bath, as you did if you were a queen 750 years ago.

Word of this reached Umm Ali, and she decided that enough was enough. And so she arranged for the Sultana to be murdered in revenge. Shajjar al-Durr was beaten to death with clogs by her own maidservants, and Umm Ali devised a rich dessert by way of celebration: for with the Atabeg and Sultana out of the way, her own son Ali was surely in line for the throne. She arranged for the sweetmeat to be handed out in the streets of Cairo and it soon became popular fare. To this day, it is known by the name of its vengeful creator: Umm Ali, and it proves that revenge is a dish that can actually be eaten either hot or cold.

Preheat the oven to 200°C/400°F/Gas mark 6.

Bake the pastry according to the instructions on the packet: this will usually involve greased baking trays, the preheated oven and 15–20 minutes cooking time, or until the pastry has risen and is golden brown. Set aside, but leave the oven on as you'll need it again.

Stir the condensed milk, water and vanilla together in a small saucepan and bring them gently to the boil. Turn down the heat and simmer for around 5 minutes. Take off the heat.

Cut the pastry into squares and assemble in a fairly large oven tray (20 x 30 x 3cm/ 8 x 13 x 1¼ in is ideal). If you are using croissants instead (and I reckon they turn out better), just pull them apart roughly with your hands and spread them over the dish. Sprinkle the coconut and your chosen nut mixture over the pastry, then drizzle the condensed milk mix over the top, taking care not to wash all the topping into one corner. Allow the milk to soak in for a few moments then spoon the whipped cream over the top.

Bake for around 15 minutes, or until the top is golden and set. Sprinkle with the nut decoration and scoff. This is best enjoyed hot (but not straight out of the oven as it is kind of burny-mouthy), but works well chilled for breakfast the next day.

Khobez Timur

DATE AND FIG BREAD

A moreish winter treat, and it's got fruit in it, so it must be good for you, yes? This is nice lightly toasted and slathered with butter or *labneh*, but it is pretty good just on its own as well. And obviously if you use a good-quality margarine instead of butter, this cake becomes vegan.

MAKES 1 'LOAF' (8–10 SLICES)

100g/3½ oz pitted dates (while Iranian Bam dates are the best in the world, slightly drier, stickier dates are better for cake-making), chopped

100g/3½ oz dried figs, chopped

250ml/9fl oz/generous 1 cup very hot Earl Grey tea (strained)

180g/6½ oz/scant 1 cup soft dark brown sugar

125g/4½ oz/generous ½ cup butter, softened

450g/1lb/scant 3¼ cups plain (all-purpose) flour (spelt works well too)

1 heaped tsp baking powder

1 tsp ground cardamom

1 tsp ground cinnamon

75g/2¾ oz/½ cup roughly chopped walnuts, plus 3–4 intact halves

Plop the dates and figs into the tea, then add the sugar. Leave for 10 minutes or so (to allow the fruit to soften and the sugar to dissolve), then add the butter, stirring so it melts in the still-warm water.

Preheat the oven to 180°C/350°F/Gas mark 4 and line a standard 1kg/2lb 4oz loaf tin with parchment paper (or greased greaseproof paper).

Sift the flour and baking powder into a bowl and add the spices and nuts. Beat in the soaked fruity mix. Spoon the mixture into the prepared tin, pressing it down so that it is evenly distributed. Push the intact walnuts into the top by way of decoration and bake for 45 minutes, or until it is firm to the touch (see Courgette and Aubergine cake, opposite). Enjoy warm or cold: if kept wrapped, this cake will keep for up to a week.

COURGETTE AND AUBERGINE CAKE

I am truly the antithesis of a domestic goddess. In fact, until a few months ago, I had never made my husband a cake. I know: you're all shocked. Anyway, he was naturally fairly excited that I had finally given in to my inner baking muse. But what did I produce for him? A sumptuous Victoria sponge? A fanciful fondant masterpiece? A manly fruitcake? Um, no, it was this: courgette and aubergine loaf. Poor lamb.

Notwithstanding my wifely failings, this is rather a good recipe, and just so very snackable. It should be pointed out that cakes, as in spongy, iced, sandwiched, cut-into-wedges type things, are rare across the Middle East, and are quite often either African or Orthodox Christian in origin, thus from Greece, Turkey, Armenia and Georgia. Having said that, incredibly ancient Babylonian tablets have been found which refer to a date-nutty-bread-cake thing called mersu. Anyway, this is inspired by something I once had in an Armenian café.

Preheat the oven to 200°C/400°F/Gas mark 6.

Prick the aubergine and bake for around 30 minutes, or until it is quite soft. Take out of the oven, cut open and leave to cool.

Grate the courgette and press it against a sieve to try and squeeze out some of its water content. Leave it to drain for 15 minutes, or so.

Next, break the eggs into your favourite cake-making bowl and beat in the sugar. Whisk vigorously for 2 minutes, although you won't be able to tell that the mixture is paling as the sugar is quite dark. Mix in the butter and oil, then beat in the dry ingredients and spices.

Once the aubergine is fairly cool, peel it carefully, retaining the skin and chop the flesh finely. Press the grated courgette against the sieve a little more to get any residual water out of the flesh, then add it to the cake mixture together with the chopped aubergine and nuts, stirring well.

Reheat the oven to 180°C/350°F/Gas mark 4. Grease a standard 1kg/2lb 4oz loaf tin and line it with greased greaseproof paper. Because grease is the word is the motion.

Carefully arrange the retained aubergine skin in the bottom of the prepared tin, then spoon the cake mixture on top, tapping the bottom of the tin so that the mixture levels itself out. Bake in the oven for around 45 minutes, then turn the oven down to 170°C/338°F/Gas mark 3 and bake for another 20–25 minutes, or until the top of the cake feels firm. To check that it is cooked through, insert a metal skewer into the middle of the cake and withdraw it – if the tip is covered in wet-looking dough, you need to cook it for another 10 minutes or so. Leave to cool slightly before turning out and peeling away the greaseproof paper.

Slice and serve warm or cold: it is pretty awesome with *labneh* (which is salted yogurt but tastes like cream cheese) spread on top. It will keep for a couple of days in an airtight container (and longer in the fridge), if you can leave it alone that long.

MAKES 1 'LOAF'
(8–10 SLICES)

1 aubergine (eggplant)

1 courgette (zucchini)

2 large eggs

125g/4½ oz/½ cup + 2 tbsp sugar (use roughly half soft brown and half caster/ superfine)

75g/2¾ oz/⅓ cup butter, melted (I use salted because I am a peasant)

50ml/1¾ fl oz/scant ¼ cup good sunflower or rapeseed (canola) oil

125g/4½ oz/scant 1 cup self-raising flour, sifted

½ tsp bicarbonate of soda (baking soda)

1 tsp ground cinnamon

½ tsp ground mace (or nutmeg at a pinch)

1 tsp ground ginger

50g/1¾ oz/½ cup flaked (slivered) almonds*

50g/1¾ oz/scant ½ cup pumpkin seed kernels*

* Nuts and seeds
You can use any other nuts you fancy: pistachios, walnuts, sunflower seed kernels, etc.

Yogurt Khavesi Tatlisi
TURKISH COFFEE AND YOGURT CAKE

Yogurt is pretty much ubiquitous in Turkish cuisine and (something like) this cake has been made in Turkey for centuries. Turkish coffee would more likely make an appearance as an accompaniment than an ingredient, but there is nothing stopping you from having one on the side as well, if you see what I mean. The cake is great on its own, but adding the syrup takes you pretty much to nirvana (and also renders it dessert material as well as teatime fodder).

MAKES A REALLY BIG CAKE
(you'll need a 25cm/10in diameter round cake tin with a fixed base or equivalent-sized square tin)

FOR THE CAKE:
400g/14oz/3 cups self-raising flour
2 tsp baking powder
1 heaped tbsp finely ground Turkish coffee
   (or strong regular ground coffee at a pinch)
1 tsp ground cardamom
250ml/9fl oz/generous 1 cup tub plain yogurt

200ml/7fl oz/generous ¾ cup honey
125g/4½ oz/generous ½ cup salted butter, melted (or use oil and a pinch of salt)
3 eggs, beaten
1 tsp vanilla essence (extract)

FOR THE SYRUP:
200g/7oz/1 cup sugar
150ml/5fl oz/⅔ cup water
juice and grated zest of 1 orange
1 heaped tsp Turkish coffee (or strong regular ground coffee at a pinch)

On yogurt

Well, the Turks are pretty sensible using as much of it as they do. Live yogurt aids the digestion and strengthens the gut. But you knew that already, yes? It is far more easily digestible than other dairy products, and so is often given to invalids or those with mild lactose intolerance. What you may not know is that it makes for one of the world's cheapest face masks (just slap it on all over, leave for 20 minutes, then wash it off again). And also that it can be the careless chef's best friend: in many commercial kitchens it is kept to hand as an instant soother for burns.

Preheat the oven to 180°C/350°F/Gas mark 4 and line the cake tin with baking parchment. Sift the first 4 ingredients into a bowl. Beat the remaining 5 cake ingredients together in another bowl, then introduce both sets of ingredients to each other, mixing well. Pour the cake mix into the prepared tin and bake for around 50 minutes, or until set on top and no longer gooey in the middle (see skewer trick on p.149).

Meanwhile, pop the syrup ingredients into a pan, bring to a gentle simmer and bubble for around 10 minutes, then set aside to cool.

When the cake is cooked, turn out and baste with the orange coffee syrup. This creation totally begs a generous dollop of crème fraîche (or, to be authentic, *kaymak*) on the side. Enjoy warm or cold. Share if you must.

Lows Iyo Sisin

SOMALIAN-STYLE SESAME SNAPS

Scholars argue as to whether sesame seeds (*simsim* in Arabic) originated in Africa or India, but scholars are always disagreeing with each other, so let's just agree that they have been in the Middle East for thousands of years. They were traded in old Mesopotamia, and cultivated extensively by the Ancient Egyptians for uses ranging from cosmetic to medicinal. The seeds are undemanding little fellows, and grow well in desert-type conditions, so it is easy to understand how their usage became so widespread.

Sesame seeds contain protein, all manner of trace minerals, vitamin B, calcium and tryptophan (which helps release serotonin, which makes you happy). The point being that this makes them practically perfect snack fodder.

They are strewn liberally across bread in countries all round the Mediterranean, and are of course the main component of both *tahina* and *halva*. In the Arabian Peninsula and East Africa, they are widely enjoyed in snack bar format: this is the best recipe I've found and comes from a consortium of my Somali customers.

MAKES AROUND 40 SQUARES, OR ENOUGH FOR A WEEK'S SNACKING

250g/9oz/generous 1 cup whole sesame seeds
200g/7oz/1 cup white sugar
100g/3½ oz/generous ¼ cup honey (about 4 tbsp)
100g/3½ oz/scant ½ cup smooth peanut butter (about 4 tbsp)
100ml/3½ fl oz/scant ½ cup date syrup (about 3½ tbsp) – if you can't find it, just use extra honey
100g/3½ oz/¾ cup desiccated (dry unsweetened) coconut

Preheat the oven to 180°C/350°F/Gas mark 4.

Spread the sesame seeds out on a fairly large baking tray and pop them into the oven for around 10 minutes, or until they assume a pleasant golden hue. Remove and set aside.

Tip, scrape and dollop the sugar, honey, peanut butter and date syrup into a saucepan and heat it through gently until the sugar has melted and everything has amalgamated.

Pour the toasted sesame seeds into the pan along with the coconut and mix thoroughly with a wooden spoon. Spread some oiled greaseproof paper over the baking tray, then spread the sesame gloop out over it, levelling it off with the wooden spoon. Place another sheet of greaseproof paper over the top: this will enable you to roll the gloop to a thickness of no more than about 2–3mm/¹⁄₁₆–⅛ in – if necessary, use 2 trays. Now score through the sesame carefully, portioning it out into snack-sized squares. Leave to cool before breaking off the squares. Store in an airtight plastic container and dish out as rewards for very good behaviour.

Badam Sokhteh

SAFFRON-SPICED CARAMELISED ALMONDS

These are a very popular Iranian sweet, and oh-so-chewy: they offer perhaps the most likely explanation as to why so many Iranians train as dentists. Something like one in five dentists in London (I've made up this statistic, but it can't be far wrong) are of Persian origin: they are clearly in cahoots with the confectionery manufacturers.

Versions of *badam sokhteh* are also made in Afghanistan and the lovely Claudia Roden refers to buying something similar in the Alexandria of her childhood.

MAKES JUST ENOUGH

200g/7oz/1 ⅓ cups shelled almonds (cashews would also respond well to this treatment)
200g/7oz/1 cup caster (superfine) sugar
½ tsp ground saffron steeped in a splash of boiling water
½ tsp ground cardamom
1 level tsp ground ginger
½ tsp salt

Preheat the oven to 170°C/340°F/Gas mark 3.

Spread the almonds out on a baking tray and roast them at for around 10 minutes, or until they have turned a more golden shade of brown.

Next, melt the sugar in a small saucepan, taking care not to let it boil. Once it has liquefied, add the saffron water, spices and salt, stirring well, then take it off the heat and tip the roasted almonds in. Now brush a non-stick baking tray with a little oil and spread the almond mixture across it. Cover with a sheet of parchment paper or some such to keep flying things off it, and set somewhere cool until it hardens.

Break into snackable pieces and store in a biscuit tin: *badam sokhteh* will keep for a few days before becoming soft.

ON DATES

It is impossible to overstate the importance of dates across the Middle East. They must have seemed like the original snack; growing in the most unlikely and hostile of conditions and offering a practically perfect shot of nutrients to fortify weary desert travellers.

They have been around since Neolithic times, and are referred to in the *Epic of Gilgamesh*, the *Egyptian Book of the Dead*, the Bible and the Koran. In the latter, they are often cited as an example of Allah's munificence; in one passage God sends them as a divine snack for the heavily pregnant Maryam (that's Mary to you):

Thereupon she conceived, and retired to a far-off place. And when she felt the pangs of childbirth she lay down by the trunk of a palm tree, crying: 'O, would that I had died and passed into oblivion.'

But a voice from above cried out to her: 'Do not despair. Your Lord has provided a brook which runs at your feet, and if you shake the trunk of this palm tree it will drop fresh ripe dates into your lap. Therefore rejoice. Eat and drink.'

In ancient times dates were credited with a seriously loopy list of health benefits, but they are undeniably a superfood, packing a punch of slow-release sugars, trace minerals, antioxidants and vitamin B. They are also reputedly quite good for the old libido...

We grow to the sound of the wind
Playing his flutes in our hair,
Palm tree daughters,
Brown flesh Badawi,
Fed with light
By our gold father;
We are loved of the free tented,
The sons of space, the
hall forgetters...
E. P. Mathers, *The 1001 Nights*

Ranginak
IRANIAN DATE 'SQUARES'

This is a classic Persian munchie, enjoyed especially during Ramadan or at times of religious significance: it is perfect for sharing, see, and it is not unusual for housewives to prepare huge trays to take to share out at the mosque. Its origins lie in the opulent court kitchens of Shiraz, however, and it can hold its own among the most lah-di-dah array of petits fours. *Ranginak* means 'colourful', and once these are all decorated they do indeed look real pretty.

Pour the oil into a pan and heat it through: then stir in the flour and cook it until it becomes quite biscuity. Take it off the heat and add the sugar, cardamom and half the cinnamon. Push a walnut half (or almond) into each date.

Now spread half the sweet roux mix out on a baking tray (one equating to 25 x 25cm/ 10 x 10in should do the trick). Layer the stuffed dates on top, then press the rest of the flour mix on top to form a smooth surface. Sprinkle the top with the ground pistachios and the rest of the cinnamon, and pop the tray into the fridge to chill. Once it is quite cold and firm, cut the *ranginak* into diamond shapes and serve with hot tea. They will keep in an airtight container for up to a week.

MAKES AROUND 30
250ml/9fl oz/generous 1 cup oil (sunflower or rapeseed/canola)
500g/1lb 2oz/3½ cups plain (all-purpose) flour (wholemeal/whole wheat is nice here, although not authentic)
125g/4½ oz/½ cup + 2 tbsp caster (superfine) sugar
1 tsp ground cardamom
2 tbsp ground cinnamon
125g/4½ oz/1¼ cups walnut halves (or whole almonds)
500g/1lb 2oz pitted Bam (or other) dates
1½ tbsp ground shelled pistachios

Dibs W'rashi

DATE SYRUP FONDUE WITH *TAHINA*

COMFORT FOOD FOR 4

2 tbsp water

2 tbsp sugar

1 tsp orange blossom water

juice and grated zest of 1 orange

100ml/3½ fl oz/scant ½ cup
    date syrup

5 tbsp *tahina*

chunks of fruit for dipping:
    strawberries, quarters of fig,
    banana, pear and apple slices,
    mandarin segments, fat grapes

Dibs W'rashi is staple fare across much of the Middle East: it is eaten with bread for breakfast or as an any-time snack and is chockful of nutritious stuff. Dibs just means syrup, and in Turkey (where it is known as *pekmez*) the dish is often made with grape or mulberry syrup instead. Pomegranate molasses also works well.

Date syrup is special: it is creamy, and has a caramel quality to it which belies its healthy and entirely natural origins. It can be used as a sweetener for pretty much any purpose, and also works well in savoury dishes. The best stuff comes from Basra in Iraq, which is where this combo originated.

To make the basic spread, just mix five parts date syrup to one part tahina, add a squeeze of lemon juice, and spread on warm bread or toast. But just for fun I decided to turn this whole thing into a fondue.

Put the water, sugar, orange blossom water and orange into a little pan and bring to the boil. Bubble for 5 minutes, then take off the heat and stir in the date syrup and tahina. Either serve straight away or pour into your very retro 1970s-style fondue pot and keep warm until needed. Arrange the fruit bits prettily on your favourite retro party platter, and dive in.

Yakh Dar Behesht

PERSIAN ANGEL DELIGHT, KIND OF

COMFORT PUDDING
FOR 6

75g/2¾ oz starch (or cornflour/
    cornstarch if you can't find it)

500ml/18fl oz/generous 2 cups
    water

50g/1¾ oz/generous ⅓ cup
    rice flour

500ml/18fl oz/generous 2 cups
    milk (use soya or rice milk
    if you like)

250g/9oz/1¼ cups sugar

5 tbsp rose water

1 tsp ground cinnamon

1 tbsp nibbed pistachios

Yakh dar behesht literally means 'ice from heaven'. This is a bit of a puzzle to me, because this light, rose-scented creation is not usually frozen at all: it is served more like a mousse, and its custardy texture means that it also works well as a layer in sweet flans or trifle.* I base my recipe on the late Roza Montazemi's version. Who is she? Kind of like a modern Iranian Mrs. Beeton. And she wrote what is possibly the biggest cookery book ever – *Honar-e-Ashpazi*.

Mix the starch with the water, then in a separate jug blend the rice flour with the milk. Pour both liquids into a heavy-bottomed pan and heat gently with the sugar and the rose water. Bring to the boil, then turn down the heat and simmer until it thickens before pouring into a basin or individual glasses. Chill, decorate with the cinnamon and nuts, and serve.

*BONUS RECIPE: 'TRIFLE' A trifling matter to prepare: soak some cake/ croissants/paklava in strong Arabic or Greek coffee (with added rum if you like that sort of thing). Layer the resultant gloop into a trifle bowl (or individual dishes). Top with *yakh dar behesht* mix, make it pretty, chill and Bobak's your uncle.

A QUARTET OF SP-ICE LOLLIES

I would love to tell you that when my stepchildren were younger I regularly created homemade ice lollies for them as they happily played in our perfectly manicured back garden. But I am totally not that organised, our kitchen is imploding, and our garden is a disgrace. These, then, have in part been created for Lewis, for I am now a wicked stepgrandmother: I will never be organised, but the kitchen might be done by the time he's five, and the garden is getting there. You can have too much halcyon anyway.

Ice lollies, popsicles, call them what you will – they are so easy to make, and even easier to eat. I rarely bother with proper lolly moulds, but rather improvise with little pots – rinsed-out yogurt pots work well. DO NOT, however, do as I did during recipe testing and improvise with an emery board for a lolly stick: this was not a good thing, no sirree. If you haven't got proper lolly sticks, cut-off wooden kebab skewers work well.

If you have the time and space, make two or three of the recipes below and overleaf: partly fill your moulds with one, freeze them, then add a layer of another mixture and so on. No one can deny that they look funky and you will earn yourself loads more wicked stepgranny points.

Each recipe makes around 10–12 lollies. Most homemade ice lollies are best eaten sooner rather than later: a week or so is the norm.

CARDAMOM COFFEE

MAKES 10–12 LOLLIES
500ml/18fl oz strong Arabic
coffee with cardamom
(you can buy it ready
blended, but if you prefer
just make strong regular
coffee with 4–5 crushed
cardamom pods)*
250g/9oz/generous 1 cup
condensed milk

Are you a kitchen bowl-licker? This recipe is worth making for the privilege thereof alone. Condensed milk. No need to say any more, right? Obviously if you are giving it to wee folk, decaff might be a better option.

Cool the coffee to room temperature, blend with the condensed milk, pour into ice cream moulds (improvised or otherwise) and freeze. If you are using non-patent moulds, don't forget to shove the lolly sticks in after an hour or so.

* You could use 450ml/
16fl oz/2 cups coffee and 50ml/
1¾ fl oz/scant ¼ cup rum.
Just saying…

SAFFRON, PISTACHIO AND ROSE-WATER CREAM

200ml/7fl oz/generous ¾ cup milk
⅓ tsp ground saffron
250g/9oz/generous 1 cup condensed milk
200ml/7fl oz/generous ¾ cup double (heavy) cream
75g/2¾ oz/½ cup shelled pistachios
5 tbsp rose water

Three of Iran's most bragged-about products all together in one frozen snack: it is an absolute classic.

Bring the milk just to boiling point in a heavy-bottomed pan and add the saffron. Allow it to steep for a few minutes before adding the condensed milk and cream. Gently bring it all to the boil, turn down the heat and simmer briefly, stirring well, before taking off the heat.

Chop the pistachios coarsely: you are aiming for something finer than a sliver, but chunkier than ground nuts. Add them to the saffron cream along with the rose water and set to chill somewhere.

When the mixture is quite cool, pour it into your chosen lolly moulds and freeze. Stir after an hour or so that the pistachio is evenly distributed.

FENNEL, MINT AND GREEN TEA

3–4 tsp green tea leaves
4 tsp fennel seeds, crushed
700ml/1¼ pints/3 cups water
big handful of fresh mint, chopped
6–7 tsp sugar

Antioxidising and an aid to digestion: this is more than just your average pop-sicle, I'm telling you. All the ingredients are measured in teaspoons because that is surely the only way to measure tea.

Add the tea leaves and crushed fennel to the water in a very clean saucepan and bring to the boil. Turn down the heat and simmer for 3–4 minutes. Take off the heat, strain, then add the mint and sugar, stirring well.

Allow to cool before pouring into moulds and freezing. After an hour, remove from the freezer and stir just to ensure that the mint is distributed evenly through the lollies.

WATERMELON, ORANGE BLOSSOM AND GINGER

750g/1lb 10oz watermelon flesh, roughly cut into chunks
120g/4oz crystallised ginger, cut into 5mm/¼ in cubes
1 tbsp orange blossom water
grated zest and juice of 1 lime
a measure or two of Cointreau give this an extra 'dimension' (optional)

So you've got fruit, fragrance, zing and bite: what more could you want from an ice lolly?

Blend (or pound) the watermelon, then whisk in the other ingredients. Pour into your moulds and freeze. Stir after an hour so that the ginger does not all congregate at the tip.

Assabee bi Loz
FINGER *PAKLAVA* WITH ALMONDS

Paklava. What's not to like? Pastry, honey, nuts. Goo, crunch, calories. Nearly everyone loves *paklava*: it's kind of addictive.

Its origins are obscure, and as is often the case with culinary innovation, most Middle Eastern countries claim to have invented it. Although there are references to desserts made with fruit and pastry and nuts in ancient Mesopotamian texts, the concept as we know and love a bit too much was almost certainly created during the heady days of Ottoman culinary supremacy. Betcha didn't know that the Topkapi Palace employed up to 800 staff in its kitchens? Or that there is a town, Gaziantep, in southeast Turkey, which is so famous for its *paklava* that they say that when the wind blows in the right direction the aroma reaches Istanbul. Anyway, the Turks certainly grew very fond of the stuff, and even had an annual *paklava* parade (the *baklava alayi*) during Ramadan when the Sultan's troops were given trays of it to share.

Sugar was rare and expensive in antiquity, and so the first confections of this nature were made with honey or *pekmez* syrup.

There are perhaps eight or nine varieties of *paklava*, and to confuse matters each country gives them different names. I offer you this one (which is Levantine in origin), as it is by far the simplest to make.

Preheat the oven to 180°C/350°F/Gas mark 4 and grease a baking tray.

Firstly, make the filling: mix the nuts, sugar, spice and flower water into a paste.

Next, cut each sheet of filo into 4 rectangles, then cover them with a damp cloth so that they don't dry out. Take 2–3 filo rectangles at a time, and brush them with a little of the melted butter. Spoon a dollop of the nut paste on to one end of each rectangle, then roll the pastry away from you, tucking in the ends as you go. Arrange the fingers on the baking tray and brush the tops with the rest of the butter. Bake for around 25 minutes, or until a pleasant golden-brown colour.

Meanwhile, make the syrup. Put the sugar, lemon and water into a pan and gently bring to the boil. Turn down the heat and simmer for 2–3 minutes then take off the heat. If you are using honey or fruit syrup, boil the water, add the honey/syrup, then take off the heat almost straight away, stirring well – the mixture otherwise turns bitter.

Allow the syrup to cool for around 30 minutes, then pour over the *assabee*.

Enjoy warm or cold. Perfect with coffee and even better with ice cream, *kaymak* or crème fraîche on top.

MAKES ABOUT
40 LITTL'UNS

FOR THE ASSABEE:
250g/9oz roughly ground
    almonds (you could of course
    also use walnuts or cashews
    or pistachios or a mixture)
100g/3½ oz/½ cup granulated
    sugar
1 tsp ground cardamom
    (optional)
2–3 tbsp rose water (or orange
    blossom water)
10 sheets filo (phyllo) pastry
    (half a standard 400g/14oz
    pack of frozen filo)
100g/3½ oz/7 tbsp melted
    butter

FOR THE SYRUP:
EITHER:
350g/12oz/½ cup caster sugar
2 tbsp lemon juice
300ml/10fl oz/1¼ cups water
OR:
300ml/10fl oz/1¼ cups water
300ml/10fl oz/1¼ cups honey
    or *pekmez* or date syrup

Samboosah Hilwah
AISHA'S YEMENI SWEET NUT PIES

**MAKES 50–60
BABY PIES**

FOR THE FILLING:
150g/5½ oz/1 cup coarsely
    chopped raw cashew nuts
75g/2¾ oz/½ cup finely
    chopped raw almonds
100g/3½ oz/½ cup caster (super-
    fine) sugar
1 tsp ground cardamom
1½ tbsp rose water

**TO MAKE THE
SAMBOOSAH:**
10 sheets filo (phyllo) pastry
    (half a standard pack of
    frozen)
oil, for frying
icing (confectioners') sugar
    and ground cardamom,
    to decorate

Samboosah, sambosic, samosa: yup, it's all the same word root/kind of stuff – exotic pies, usually made to sell in the street. These are well-known Arabian street fare, although among my Somali and Yemeni customers they are most often cooked as comfort food, for a taste of 'back home'.

Aisha is half Somali, half Yemeni, incredibly beautiful and (considering she has four children under six) astonishingly serene. She is also a very good cook. Her English is getting better, but when she first came into the shop we used to have a lot of fun as she tried to mime the various spices she wanted.

Mix the nuts, sugar and spice together, then add the rose water: the mixture should bind into a paste. If it seems a little crumbly still, add a splash of cold water.

Cut each sheet of filo into strips lengthways: standard filo width is around 36cm/14¼in, so I usually aim for five 7cm/2¾in strips out of each sheet. But you may manage six 6cm/2½in strips. Cover the filo with a wet cloth so that it doesn't dry out while you're working. Lay one strip at a time on the work surface in front of you, short side facing you. Place a teaspoon of the nut mix in one corner of the strip, then fold the pastry over so that the mixture is enclosed in a small triangular pocket. Next fold that triangle over, up the strip, then fold it back across again. Repeat all the way up to the top. Moisten your fingers with some water and squeeze the pastry edges together to seal. Do the same with all the filo strips.

Heat 3–4cm/1¼–1½in of oil in a heavy-bottomed pan (or use a deep-fat fryer with clean oil) until it is sizzle hot (but you don't want it smoking). Fry off the pastries in batches, scooping them out once they are golden brown. Drain them on a piece of kitchen paper. Leave to cool a little before stealing one, as the centre of these things gets really hot.

When cool(er), dredge with a little icing sugar mixed with cardamom and serve with spiced tea or Arabic coffee. *Sahtein*! (Now you know how to say *bon appétit* in Arabic.)

I serve these with crème fraîche and some barberry coulis and they are ace. What's that? You'd like my recipe for barberry coulis too? Oh all right then…

BARBERRY AND LIME COULIS

MAKES 200ML/7FL OZ/¾ CUP
125g/4½ oz barberries, picked through and
    washed (or use redcurrants, or cranberries)
400ml/14fl oz/1¾ cups water

2 tbsp sugar
juice and grated zest of 2 limes
1 heaped tsp ground fennel seeds
2cm/¾ in fresh ginger, peeled and chopped

Put the barberries in a pan together with the water and all the other ingredients. Bring to the boil and reduce by roughly half, stirring from time to time. Press through a sieve and cool. Drizzle over *faloodeh* (Persian noodle sorbet), or tarts, or anything you like really.

Booza

MASTIC ICE CREAM WITH PISTACHIOS

Booza is THE ice cream to eat in the streets of Arabistan, especially Syria, whence it hales. In some countries, it is actually sold as ice lollies, in others it is served in paper cups. It's all kind of gloopy, like Indian *kulfi* or Persian *bastani*, and this is mostly due to the addition of *mastic* (see note on p.54) and *sahlab* (an orchid extract). As this latter is almost impossible to find (except as an ingredient in other things), I have substituted cornflour.

MAKES ENOUGH
FOR 4 PEOPLE
3 tbsp cornflour (cornstarch)
750ml/1¼ pints/3⅓ cups full-fat (whole)
    milk (oat milk works well too if you want
    a vegan/dairy-free version)
160g/5¾ oz/scant 1 cup sugar

⅓ tsp (i.e. 4–5 granules) mastic
1½ tbsp flower water (rose, orange blossom
    or a mixture of both)
100g/3½ oz/ ⅔ cup nibbed pistachios
2–3 tbsp fresh pomegranate kernels (optional:
    use fresh redcurrants or dried cranberries
    instead if you like, or just leave them out)

Put the cornflour into a small bowl and add around 5 tablespoons of the milk, stirring well to get rid of any lumps. Pour the rest of the milk into a pan along with most of the sugar and warm gently. When it is fairly hot but not boiling, add a splash of the warm liquid to the cornflour, mixing well once again, then tip the whole lot into the pan.

Next, pulverise the mastic with the remaining sugar (if you don't have a pestle and mortar, wrap it in a clean cloth and bash it with your rolling pin) and add it to the hot milk along with the flower water. Bring to the point of boiling, stirring constantly, then take off the heat. Allow to cool completely before pouring into a suitable freezeable container (or your ice-cream maker if you have such a grand thing). Freeze for about 45 minutes, then take it out of the freezer and churn well. At this stage, stir in the pistachios and pomegranate seeds, then put the whole lot back to freeze hard.

Remove from the freezer 5–10 minutes before serving decorated with more pistachios, or pomegranate kernels, or rose petals, or all three.

Dolmeh Shirin

PUDDING *DOLMEH*

In theory anything that is stuffed (we're talking cooking, not taxidermy: civet *dolmeh* would just be silly) can be called a *dolmeh*. So it kind of makes sense to extend this to the realm of sweet snacks too. Most importantly, the next three recipes are fun. And cooking is getting a little bit too serious, don't you think?

SWEET-STUFFED LETTUCE LEAVES

There are serious stuffed leafy things (usually vine leaves or cabbage leaves). And then there are these stuffed leafy things: romaine lettuce leaves wrapped around a fragrant rice and fruit stuffing served with date syrup cream.

Boil the rice until just cooked, refresh under cold water and leave to drain for 30 minutes.

Fill a bowl with really cold water and park it near your cooker. Next bring a pan of water to the boil and blanch the 30 pretty lettuce leaves a few at a time: they only need around 45 seconds. Remove them from the pan and plunge them into the cold water – this will stop them from becoming mushy and unworkable – before leaving them to drain in a colander. At this stage, drain the raisins and apricots as well.

Tip the drained rice into a bowl and add the saffron together with the raisins, apricots, other spices, fruit and nuts. Mix well.

Take a lettuce leaf and put it on the work surface in front of you, stalky end pointing away from you. Place a dessertspoon of the rice mixture at the end of the leaf nearest you, dot a tiny cube of butter on top and roll the leaf away from you, tucking the side bit in as you roll so that the filling ends up completely encased in lettuce. Repeat with the other leaves.

Invert a plate (preferably not your best china) in the base of a heavy-bottomed pan, and scatter any substandard lettuce leaves across it. Arrange the *dolmeh* in a circle, working from the outside in, piling them up if necessary, and dot any remaining butter on top. Add the rose water, *pekmez* and lemon juice, then invert another plate on top. Add enough cold water to the pan so that you can just see it, and bring to the boil before turning down the heat and simmering gently. You will need to cook the lettuce leaves for around 15 minutes: once this time has elapsed, take off the heat and leave it somewhere to cool a little.

Heat the cream gently in a small pan until it is just short of boiling, then take it off the heat and add the date syrup. Serve the *dolmeh* hot, warm or cold with the sauce in a jug alongside. These are so moreish you might have to hide them from yourself.

MAKES 30

150g/5½ oz/¾ cup basmati (or long-grain) rice
30 nice romaine (cos) lettuce leaves (2 heads of lettuce), retain any less pristine leaves
50g/1¾ oz/⅓ cup raisins, soaked
50g/1¾ oz/generous ¼ cup dried apricots, chopped and soaked
pinch of ground saffron steeped in boiling water
½ tsp ground cinnamon
½ tsp ground ginger
¼ tsp ground mace (or nutmeg)
100g/3½ oz dates, pitted and chopped
50g/1¾ oz/⅓ cup pine nuts (or sunflower seed kernels)
50g/1¾ oz/⅓ cup pistachio kernels, roughly chopped (or almonds, or hazelnuts)
5 tbsp butter, cut into pieces
2 tbsp rose water
2 tbsp *pekmez* (grape syrup) or pomegranate paste
1 tbsp lemon juice
150ml/5fl oz/⅔ cup single (light) cream
3 tbsp date syrup (or molasses)

SWEETSHOP-STUFFED TANGERINES

A TRICK TO PLAY
ON 12 CHILDREN

12 tangerines (or mandarins,
    or clementines...)
½ small pineapple, peeled
    and cut into small chinks
4 kiwi fruits, peeled and cut
    into small chunks (of course,
    you can use any fruit that is
    not too soft)
½ tsp ground cardamom
juice of 1 small lemon
2 tsp orange blossom water
12 small pieces of *gaz* (Persian
    nougat, but any nougat is
    fine), cut into 1cm/½ in cubes
200g/7oz *halva*, cut into
    1cm/½ in cubes
16 pieces of rose or orange
    Turkish delight, cut into
    1cm/½ in cubes
2 small tubes of sherbet (I found
    some under the name of
    Rainbow Dust, which sounds
    like it ought to be illegal)

Ameliaranne Stiggins* goes east. These stuffed fruit are great fun, easy to assemble and very popular with the under 10s and the over 23s. They are also pretty healthy, as after-school/party treats go.

Cut the top off each of the tangerines, and use a small pointy knife to prize the fruit away from the peel, taking care not to damage the latter. If the skin is baggy, then you can probably extract the fruit fairly easily with your fingers; if it is taut, then you will need to cut the segments out. Reserve the hollowed-out skins/tops and cut the tangerine pieces into chunks (removing any pips along the way).

    Add the pineapple and kiwi to the tangerine in a bowl. Mix the cardamom with the lemon juice and flower water and pour it over the chopped fruit, mixing gently. Cover and set aside. Mix the nougat, *halva* and Turkish delight cubes in another bowl.

    When you are ready to serve, put a little of the confectionery mix in the bottom of each tangerine, followed by a layer of fruit, followed by more sweets and then top them with another layer of fruit (along with some of the juice). At the last minute, trickle some of the sherbet over each one, and recover them with the tangerine tops so that the fruit looks more or less whole. Keep a straight face as you serve them, reminding disappointed small people that in Ameliaranne's day tangerines were a treat. This one should earn you lots of bonus Wonka points.

Ameliaranne Stiggins and the Green Umbrella is a wonderful children's book written in 1920 by Constance Heward. The eponymous heroine, whose family is very poor, goes to a party and tries to bring back all of her food – cakes, tangerines, sweets – hidden in her umbrella to feed her ailing brothers and sisters. It made me think that maybe cakes and sweets hidden in a tangerine might be fun.

DATES STUFFED WITH SPICED *LABNEH*

MAKES 50

150g/5½ oz/ ⅔ cup creamed
    labneh (or thick plain yogurt
    blended with ½ tsp salt)
¼ tsp ground cumin
½ tsp sumac
¼ tsp ground cinnamon
¼ tsp chilli powder (optional)
50 dates (soft ones, such as
    Iranian Bam or Medjool)
25 walnut halves (or 50 quarters)

So easy, but such a great thing to have in the fridge: they offer instant energy. I should warn you that this is the one thing that is never left over on *meze* spreads, so keep some back for yourself right from the beginning.

Blend the *labneh* with the spices, mixing well. Pit the dates, taking care to split them down one side only, and split the walnut halves. Fill each date with *labneh* and poke a walnut on top. Arrange prettily on a platter.

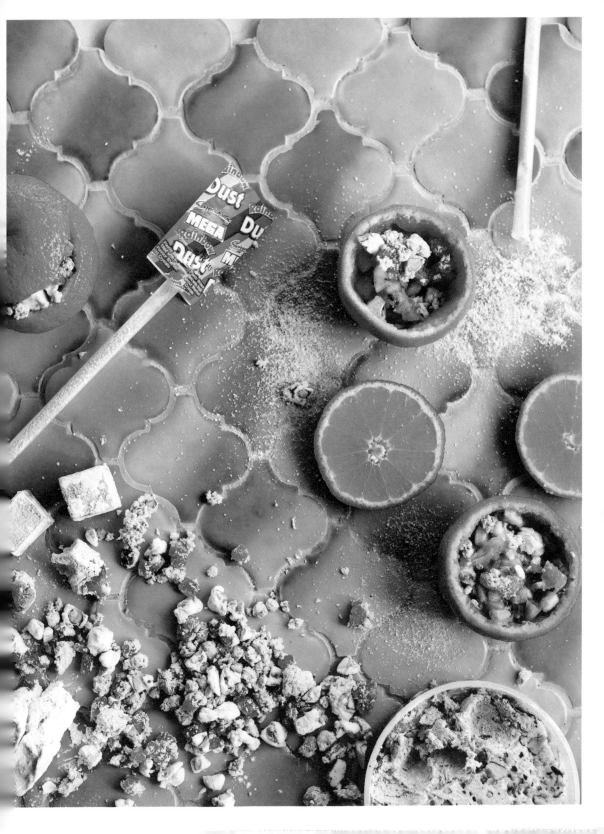

PUDDING *MEZE*

You know how you often want everything on the dessert menu, and then you agree with your mates that you'll each try something different and share it, and then they won't share with you? Or when you're having a bit of a soirée and the conversation drops away because everyone is cramming cake into their mouths? Well, this idea gets round the problem. Chuck everything in the middle and let them get on with it. Share. Keep it informal. Keep the chatter going. Much better.

So what should you put on the table? The stuffed lettuce leaves and dates on pp.165, 166 are a good place to start. In my book *Veggiestan* I offered a recipe for sweet houmous, made with *tahina*, honey, cinnamon and cardamom. You can make something like *tsatsiki* by blending yogurt with honey, kiwi fruit or melon and chopped fresh mint. And a chillied fruit salsa (finely diced fruit dressed with rose water, chilli, sugar and lime) with sweetened mascarpone.

Fresh fruit for dipping is an obvious addition, but fruit or sweet vegetable crisps are a lot more fun...

QUINCE CRISPS

MAKES ENOUGH FOR
A PARTY BOWLFUL
75g/2¾ oz/¼ cup + 2 tbsp
   granulated sugar
1 tsp ground cinnamon
½ tsp ground nutmeg
½ tsp ground ginger
1 fat quince
   (around 300g/10½ oz)

You can, of course, use all sorts of fruit and veg to make these sweet crisps: sweet potato, beetroot, carrot, apple, pear, firm mango...

Preheat the oven to its lowest setting, and line a large baking tray or 2 smaller ones with parchment paper.

Mix the sugar with the spices. Peel and core* the quince and slice into very fine slices (with a mandoline if you have one), and spread them out over the baking tray(s). Sprinkle the spiced sugar over the fruit as evenly as possible, and bake for around 1½ hours, or until slightly browned and kind of crispy. Remove from the oven and peel off the parchment paper: the crisps will get crisper as they cool.

Quince crisps will keep for a few days in an airtight container.

* An Iranian housewife would retain the quince seeds as they are one of the best natural remedies for chesty coughs. Make a decoction of them, adding honey if necessary, and sip as tea.

SWEET *TABOULEH*

Salad is a must for most *meze* spreads. You can always make up a good fruit salad or you could push the *dhow* out and make a special sweet salad. This stuff hits the mark at practically any time of day and makes for a super-nutritious breakfast.

MEZE FOR 8 OR
BREAKFAST FOR 4

150g/5½ oz assorted diced dried fruit (prunes, dates, figs, apricot, mango) or use diced fresh fruit (strawberries, banana, kiwi, pomegranate seeds, grapes …)

300g/10½ oz/generous 2 cups medium bulghur wheat

400ml/14fl oz/1¾ cups very hot Earl Grey tea made with 6 tsp sugar

150g/5½ oz/1 cup assorted nut kernels: sunflower seeds, pumpkin seeds, hemp seeds, chopped pistachios, pine nuts

1 tbsp toasted sesame oil
2 tsp runny honey
1 tbsp raspberry vinegar
1 tbsp lime juice
big handful of fresh mint, shredded
big handful of fresh coriander (cilantro), chopped
few sprigs of fresh basil, chopped

If using dried fruit, soak for around 30 minutes then drain.

Meanwhile, spread the bulghur wheat out on a deep oven tray and pour the tea over it, stirring well. Cover with a clean kitchen paper or piece of foil and leave for about 10 minutes. At the end of this time, use a fork to fluff it up.

When it has cooled more or less to room temperature, add the fruit and nuts, mixing well. Whisk the oil, honey vinegar and lime juice together and drizzle through the bulghur wheat, checking that the 'seasoning' (sweetness) is to your liking. Finally, stir in the chopped herbs. Prepare to amaze your guests.

 Note

Wheat- or gluten-intolerant? A very good *tabouleh* can be made with millet, but you will need to boil the grains in the tea rather than just soaking them – it will take about half an hour to cook, and you will need to add at least 100ml/3½ fl oz/½ cup extra water.

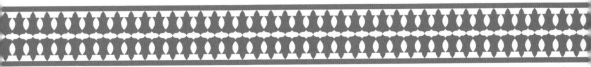

Something To
Wash It Down

ORANGE BLOSSOM AND MINT LEMONADE

**MAKES A 2 LITRE/
3½ PINT/8 CUP JUG**
500g/1lb 2oz/2½ cups sugar
1 litre/1¾ pints/4 cups water
3 tbsp orange blossom water
10 nice fat lemons
big handful of fresh mint,
    shredded
sparkling water (or still) to top up
mint leaves, lemon slices,
    cucumber slices to serve

There is no excuse for buying that nasty fizzy stuff that goes by the name of lemonade: the real thing is easy to make, even with a manual juicer.

This drink is a variation on the classic idea of *sharbat*, a sweetened fruit drink common to most Middle Eastern countries. The concept seems to have evolved in the seventh and eighth centuries, which is roughly when the advent of Islam put the kibosh on drinking more intoxicating beverages. Iced *sharbat* of one variety or another is available from street vendors: particularly popular are quince, sour cherry, orange and rose.

Our exotic lemonade has it all: a hint of floral sweetness, a soupçon of intriguing freshness, and a big hit of fragrant sharpness. Gosh: so many adjectives in such a small sentence. Without wanting to sound like an advert for a second-grade supermarket chain any further, this drink packs it all for sweaty summer day refreshment. One glass is never enough.

Make syrup by boiling the sugar and water together. Once the sugar has all dissolved, add the blossom water and take it off the heat.

Next, scrub the lemons before zesting 5 of them and juicing all of them. Add both the zest and the juice to the cooling syrup. Once the mixture is quite cool, add the shredded mint to it, and pop it in a covered container in the fridge to chill.

Serve it over ice in your prettiest perfect-housewife jug, topped up according to taste with sparkling water, and made irresistible with the finishing touches of extra slices of lemon, mint leaves and cucumber. Stand back and marvel at your own domesticity.

KASHMIRI TAMARIND COOLER

Tamarind originated in India, and our name for it reflects that: the Arabs called it *Tamr Hindi* (Indian dates) as they weren't quite sure what it was at first. Indeed the tamarind is the Zaphod Beeblebrox of the fruit world: compellingly weird to look at, and full of surprisingly good stuff. It is famously cooling, packed with phytochemicals (the secret police of the nutrient world) and vitamins and trace minerals and fibre.

   This recipe comes courtesy of my (Kashmiri) butcher's mother-in-law.

MAKES 750ML/25FL OZ/
GENEROUS 3 CUPS

300g/10½ oz block of tamarind (or use same weight of fresh, peeled pods,* or 2 tbsp tamarind paste)

750ml/25fl oz/generous 3 cups boiling water

juice and grated zest of 2 limes

2cm/¾in piece fresh ginger, peeled and chopped

2 cloves

6 cracked peppercorns

2 cinnamon sticks

250g/9oz/1¼ cups brown sugar (traditionally jaggery, which is whole sugar formed into a cone)

Put the tamarind in a pan and pour the boiling water over it. Turn the heat on underneath the pan and continue to simmer gently, stirring from time to time, until the tamarind has more or less dissolved. Add the lime juice, zest and spices, and cook for a further 10 minutes before turning the heat off and adding the sugar. Stir well and leave to steep for a further 20 minutes.

   Next, press the whole lot through a sieve, pushing to get as much juice as possible from the pulp. Bottle the resulting syrup until needed.

   Serve in brown-sugar-frosted glasses, over ice, topped up with ginger ale or soda or just plain ol' water. Also reputedly 'wicked' in cocktails (according to a local barman).

✳ Note on tamarind

Hmm... Pods. Well, you need to flake the outer husk away, then peel off the inner stringy stuff, and pop out the seeds in the middle. The black gooey substance remaining is your edible tamarind. Handy hint: do not casually toss the pips in the dying embers of an open fire: they explode (as do lychee stones).

Sharbat Amardine

APRICOT PASTE CORDIAL

**MAKES 1 LITRE/
1¾ PINTS/4 CUPS**
500g/1lb 2oz amardine (or
   the same quantity of dried
   apricots), cut into small chunks
1 litre/1¾ pints/4 cups water
sugar, to taste

A lovely creamy fruity drink which works hot or cold. This is a comforting Ramadan special, made both at home and sold by street vendors, but to my mind it is far too good to be reserved for just one month a year.

Amardine is apricot fruit leather, and is available in most Middle Eastern stores now – but if you can't find it, just use good-quality dried apricots instead. Dried apricots are enjoyed throughout the Middle East, in tagines and stews, and in all sorts of creative ways. Try to find the Iranian variety known as *khaysi*, fresh or dried: the flavour is astonishing, like honey. I don't know what they are called in English, but just in case any of you are botany geeks, my Latin/Farsi horticultural dictionary gives the Latin name as *Armeniaca duhamel*.

Soak the amardine, preferably overnight.

Once the amardine has soaked for a goodly while, pour the whole lot into a pan and bring to the boil slowly, stirring from time, until the mix looks quite homogenised. If you are using dried apricots, a brief whizz in the blender would be beneficial at this stage. Add sugar (or honey) to taste: a squirt of fresh lemon or a splash of orange blossom water may also be added to lend extra oomph.

Enjoy hot (this rocks with a swirl of cream), or chill and have cold. I reckon this has good potential as a cocktail mixer, but at the time of writing this remains untried.

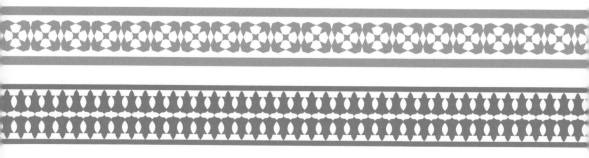

Karkade

HIBISCUS TEA

Hibiscus crops up all over the place: some nations call it roselle, while in my part of the world (Peckham) folks are more likely to use its West Indian name: sorrel. But the country that can really claim it as its own is Egypt, and this drink's popularity goes back to the time of the pharaohs.

Regardless of whether they were actually aliens from another planet or not, those pharaoh chaps really were pretty astute, as a lot of their favoured comestibles are incredibly healthy. Hibiscus is full of antioxidants, but it seems to be particularly good for those with diabetes and high blood pressure.

Put the flowers in a pan or heatproof jug, add the water, sweeten to taste and leave to steep and cool for around 8 hours, or overnight. Strain and bottle. This will keep for a couple of weeks in the fridge. *Karkade* is most often enjoyed over ice in hot countries (kind of figures, yes?), but it is lovely as a hot drink. A word of warning – while you're admiring its deep red hue, remember that it stains…

MAKES 1 LITRE/
1 ¾ PINTS/4 CUPS
30g/1oz hibiscus flower heads/
    petals (fresh or dry)
1 litre/1¾ pint/4 cups boiling
    water
honey or sugar, to taste

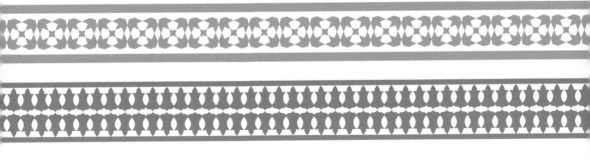

FLOWER POWER:
ROSE, BORAGE AND MARSHMALLOW TEA

Flower tea is nothing new. We've been drinking camomile and jasmine tea in the West for a long time. But this trio of teas is relatively unknown, rather pleasant and comprises some potent store cupboard remedies to boot. While these are not exactly street foods, they are doled out by *hakims* (or street doctors) in Afghanistan and Central Asia, and made all over the region as soothing medicinal compounds.

You can make flower tea from fresh or dried flowers, but it goes without saying that if you are using the former, find some organic ones if possible, or at least forage away from busy roads. You also need to make very sure you are picking the right thing.

Once you have sourced your petals, wash them in cold water then steep them in boiling water for around 8–10 minutes. A tea ball helps, but you can just make it loose in a mug or teapot. Strain the tea if you like, and add honey (or sugar) to taste.

Rose petal tea has a delectable aroma and a curiously fruity flavour. It is full of vitamin C, helps flush the kidneys, detoxes the urinary system and reputedly soothes the nerves. Iranians drink it 'to prevent coughs and colds'.

Borage (*Borago officinalis*) tea is also good for winter snuffles, acting as a demulcent for stubborn coughs. It is also touted as a remedy for insomnia, depression, premenstrual syndrome (PMT) and anxiety.

Marshmallow (*Althaea officinalis*) tea – not to be confused with the wondrous, spongy sweets on which we burn our mouths at bonfire parties. Marshmallow has a pleasant flavour and packs a punch of goodness. It is a powerful demulcent, helping to relieve congestion on the chest and, um, down below. It is also said to be highly efficacious in the relief of sore throats.

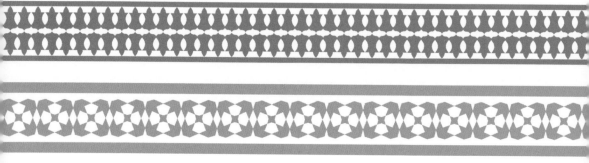

Chai Karak

SPICED TEA

The word *chai* just means tea in most Indo-European languages, and so the rise of the term 'chai tea' in the West causes much merriment, as it effectively means 'tea tea' (in the same way *na'an* just means bread, and so *'na'an* bread' is 'bread bread').

Anyway, the idea of drinking spiced white tea evolved during colonial times in India and kind of spread out from there. Arabs and Iranians are fond of black tea with cardamom, or bergamot, or rose petals, but most would not dream of adding such a heady mix as our recipe below, and the idea of adding milk to tea is quite abhorrent to them. But fancy tea bars in the bigger towns are starting to purvey fancy teas, and this spiced tea is already popular in East Africa.

Put the water and milk in a pan together with the spices and bring to the boil. Turn down the heat and simmer for 5 minutes, then stir in the tea and take off the heat. Cover the pan and allow to brew for a further 5 minutes.

To serve, fish out the cinnamon sticks and strain the tea into two cups, sweetening to taste. Slide one of the rescued cinnamon sticks into each cup and enjoy. Particularly good next to a roaring log fire, or in a candlelit bath.

TEA FOR 2

300ml/10fl oz/1¼ cups water

200ml/7fl oz/generous ¾ cup full-fat (whole) milk

1cm/½ in piece fresh ginger, peeled and grated

1 star anise

2 cinnamon sticks

6 cardamom pods, lightly crushed

4 peppercorns, lightly crushed

3 cloves

2 tsp black tea

sugar, to taste

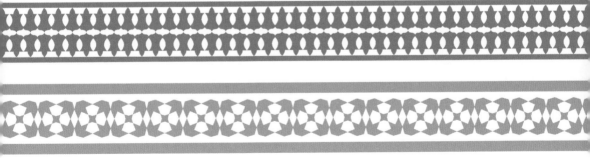

ICED TURKISH DELIGHT COFFEE

A worried anxious person is a wretched person; he perishes away with grief. Let him drink our Effendi's coffee, let it intoxicate him, free him of his troubles...
(ascribed to Rumi)

The Turks take their coffee very seriously, but this recipe is more about frivolity and sweetness. It is just like regular iced coffee, but with a far darker heart. The drink hits you with its alluring aroma, and then caresses your tongue (did I just write that?) with exotic, fruity after-notes. Look: it's really good. And filling: a quaffable snack. Carob is an optional but delectable extra: blackstrap molasses or date syrup could also be used, or you could of course just use sugar.

MAKES 1 LITRE/
1¾ PINTS/4 CUPS
20 cubes pistachio Turkish delight
5 Turkish coffee cups of water (about
    375ml/13fl oz/1⅔ cups)
5 heaped tsp ground Turkish
    (or Greek) coffee
2–3 split cardamom pods

2 tbsp carob syrup (or use carob powder:
    see feature on p.185)
500ml/18fl oz/generous 2 cups milk
    (soya, rice, oat or almond all work well
    too)
a big scoop of ice cubes (about 200ml/7fl oz/
    generous ¾ cup)

Quarter the cubes of Turkish delight, spread it out on a tray, and pop it in the freezer for 2–3 hours.

Put the water in a small pan and add the coffee and cardamom, stirring well. Bring the liquid just to the point of boiling: as it starts to rise up the sides of the pan, take it off the heat (if you leave it beyond this the coffee acquires a burnt flavour). Stir in the carob syrup and set aside to cool a little before straining through muslin (or some of that tough kitchen paper); a super-fine sieve will do at a pinch. Add the milk, whisking well.

When you are ready to serve, wrap the frozen Turkish delight and ice in a very clean tea towel and beat the hell out of it (or use a blender if you possess a sturdy model). Tip the crushed ice into 4 glasses and top up with the coffee.

In winter: forget all that ice. Make the coffee/carob combo, strain it and add hot milk. Place a spoonful of chopped (non-frozen) Turkish delight in the bottom of each glass or mug, and pour the hot coffee over it. The *loukoum* doesn't exactly melt, but it does become wondrously gloopy. Serve with a long spoon and a smile.

MOROCCAN AVOCADO SMOOTHIE

MAKES 2 GLASSES

1 large ripe avocado, skinned
    and stoned
500ml/18fl oz/generous 2 cups
    milk (almond works well
    here, but any will do)
2 tbsp ground almonds
2 tsp orange flower water
3 tsp icing (confectioners') sugar
1 scoop ice cubes
slices of orange, to garnish

I once trumped a very snotty head chef by producing avocado ice cream as a dessert (lowly sous chefs aren't meant to be that creative). I paid for it in washing up of course. The thing is, avocados are so creamy they just demand to be used in sweet recipes as well as savoury.

This is not my invention but a well-established Moroccan drink.

Put the avocado in your blender (or chop it and then force it through a sieve) with a little of the milk and whizz until creamy. Add the rest of the ingredients and blend. Pour into two glasses, garnish and enjoy.

MELON AND ROSEWATER SMOOTHIE

MAKES 2 GLASSES

1 small ripe melon (Galia or
    Ogen are perfect), peeled
    and deseeded
2 tbsp rose water
grated zest and juice of ½ a lime
1 scoop of ice cubes
few dried rose petals, to garnish
    (optional)

This Persian classic is a lovely free-from-everything recipe. Melons are eaten by the bucket in Iran in summer as they are naturally cooling. The West might just have discovered the marketable power of the smoothie, but Iranians have been making the things since forever.

While this makes a lovely drink as it is, I also like to freeze it so it becomes just solid and serve it as a kind of *semifreddo* to cleanse the palate between courses (only when I am showing off, of course).

Pop the melon in a blender along with the rose water, lime and ice and whizz until smooth-ish. Pour into two glasses and garnish with rose petals, if you like.

BONUS RECIPE: WATERMELON SMOOTHIE

You can also make a wicked watermelon smoothie by blending chunks of watermelon with raspberries, mint, lime, a hint of chilli and pomegranate molasses.

BARBERRY JUICE

This is real Persian street fare: to be honest, I've come across few Iranians who make it at home, and yet they all have childhood memories of drinking the stuff in sweltering summer streets and bazaars. There is apparently nothing quite like it for cooling the blood...

Barberries are astonishingly good for you: they are full of vitamin C and are used by herbalists to treat diabetes, renal problems (red stuff is generally good for the kidneys) and dodgy digestion. They do grow in the UK, and feature in many Victorian cookery books (wherein they were mostly used to make jelly).

This recipe was shouted at me by sundry tiny aunties-in-law all the way from Kermanshah (via Skype). Technology is occasionally a wonderful thing.

Pick through the barberries – they live up to their name and can be full of barbs and bits of twig – and wash them thoroughly. Tip them into a pan, add the water and bring to the boil. Turn down the heat and simmer for around 20 minutes, then sweeten to taste and press through a fine sieve. Cool then chill until required – the juice should keep for up to a week.

MAKES 500ML/
18FL OZ/2 CUPS
200g/7oz barberries
(dried or fresh)
500ml/18fl oz/generous
2 cups water
2 tbsp sugar (optional)

ON CAROB

Most of you probably know that carob is used as a chocolate substitute, and that it grows in alien-looking pods. It is awesome: naturally sweet, and (dare I say it) with much more fragrance and taste than cocoa. It is also caffeine-free and full of calcium. I have always used carob syrup, which is widely available in Greek, Turkish and Middle Eastern shops, but carob powder may be easier to source. Use it as a sweetener, or in marinades, salad dressings and baking. Or mix with *tahina*.

What a lot of you won't know is that the carob (which also uses the pseudonyms locust bean and St. John's bread) is also a notable little fellow because he gave us our unit of measurement, the carat: the Latin word (derived from Greek, like so many things) for him is *Ceratonia siliqua*. The carob bean is apparently consistent in mass, and thus came to be used as a weight for precious stones and gold.

Useless information of the day: because if you put all the useless information together it amounts to a life of dedicated geekery. *Faal* or divination is very popular across the Middle East. It can imply anything from horoscopes to palm-reading and the old Rosy tea leaves (and Kourosh coffee grouts). An astonishing number of our Cypriot and Middle Eastern friends practise it.

If you want to read your grouts, drink your coffee then invert the cup over the saucer. Wait for 5 minutes, and peer at the results. Both the patterns in the cup and on the saucer can be 'analysed', and you should look for images both in the grouts and the spaces between the grouts. An apple is a sign of achievement, birds and fish and trees are mostly good things, cats mean treachery, dogs fidelity, faces indicate change… Well, that's just to start you off. A lot of it is intuitive.

And by the way, the art of reading beverage dregs is collectively known as tasseography. You will thank me for telling you that one day.

index

bibliography

This is a list of books to which I refer constantly and keep in an untidy sprawl next to my desk.

FOOD

Claudia Roden, *A New Book of Middle Eastern Food* (London, Penguin Books, 1968) – the undisputed doyenne of Middle Eastern food writers

Helen Saberi, *Noshe Djan* (London, Prospect Books, 1986) – remains unsurpassed on the subject of Afghan cooking

Margaret Shaida, *The Legendary Cuisine of Persia* (Grub Street, 1992) – the first lady to write a Persian cookbook in English

Rena Salaman, *Greek Food* (Fontana Paperbacks, 1983) – in my opinion the best work on Greek food, sparkling with warmth and humour

Tess Mallos, *The Complete Middle Eastern Cookbook* (Hardie Grant Books, 1979/2012) – an astonishingly complete and authoritative round up, now delightfully back in print

Paula Wolfert, *The Food of Morocco* (Bloomsbury, 2012) – just a lovely, lovely book

Nevin Halici, *Sufi Cuisine* (London, Saqi, 2005)

HISTORY

Jean Bottero, *The Oldest Cuisine in the World* (University of Chicago Press, 2004) – proof that fine dining really isn't a new thing

Rodinson, Arberry and Perry, *Medieval Arab Cookery* (London, Prospect Books, 2001) – the most complete medieval work of reference on Arabic cuisine

[edited by] Sami Zubaida and Richard Tapper, *A Taste of Thyme* (I.B. Tauris and Co. Ltd, 1994) – a collection of fascinating essays on culinary history in the Middle East

HERBAL LORE

Dr. Sohrab Khoshbin, *Giahan Mojezegar* (Miraculous Herbs) (Tehran, Nashreh Salez, 2005) – this volume is in Farsi; the book is reputedly now available in English from the good doctor's Canadian website: www.drkhoshbin.com

V. Mozaffarian, *Dictionary of Iranian Plant Names: Latin, English, Persian* (Tehran, Farhang Moaser, 1996)

BY THE SAME AUTHOR

You know, just in case you've enjoyed this book...

Sally Butcher, *Persia in Peckham* (Prospect Books, 2007) – more of the same as this, but with a heavy Persian bias and a lot of anecdotes

Sally Butcher, *Veggiestan* (Pavilion, 2011) – a vegetable lover's tour of the Middle East

WEBSITES

And finally a couple of really helpful websites...
For herbal lore and fancy plant names: www.pfaf.org

For its simply huge archive of articles on Arabistan and beyond: www.saudiaramcoworld.com

acknowledgements

A cookery book is a culinary autobiography, built over many years and through interactions with countless people, both chef-shaped and otherwise. It would be impossible to acknowledge all of those who have helped create it. But I will endeavour so to do nevertheless.

Firstly an enormous thank you to everyone at Anova Books, especially editress Emily Preece Morrison. The behind-the-scenes team are some of the loveliest people with whom I have had the pleasure to work: thanks are thus due to Yuki, the nice photo lady; Valerie, food stylist extraordinaire; Wei, for practically perfect props; Georgie, for brave and bold design; and last-but-not-least, Kom in PR. I am also indebted to Kathy, the copy editor, for her i-dotting, t-crossing and conversions.

I am indebted once again to my wonderful agent, Veronique Baxter, and her assistant Laura for their faith and patience.

I am also grateful to the team of loyal customers and friends who have tested, tasted and tweaked the recipes, and from whom I have drawn inspiration.

I would also like to give special mention to my team of very supportive BFFs and fellow '63 babies: Caroline, Cathy, Fiona, Jan, Kate, and Lisette, not forgetting Claire and Russell – happy birthday year, guys.

Lastly: hugs and thanks to my (bestest supporter/sternest critic) mother, and my better half, Jamshid.

Sally
Peckham, 2013

This edition published in the United Kingdom in 2020 by Pavilion
43 Great Ormond Street
London, WC1N 3HZ

www.pavilionbooks.com

ISBN: 978-1-911641-66-7

A CIP catalogue record for this book is
available from the British Library

Commissioning editor: Emily Preece-Morrison
Design and art direction: Georgina Hewitt
Layout: Allan Sommerville
Photographer: Yuki Sugiura
Home economist: Valerie Berry
Stylist: Wei Tang
Copy editor: Kathy Steer
Indexer: Ruth Ellis

10 9 8 7 6 5 4 3 2 1

Reproduction by Mission, Hong Kong
Printed by Toppan Leefung Printing Ltd, China

NOTES
1 teaspoon = 5ml; 1 tablespoon = 15ml.
Both metric and imperial measures are given for the recipes.
Follow either set of measures, not a mixture of both, as they are not
interchangeable.